GOD'S WORD FOR HEALING & WHOLENESS

GOD'S WORD FOR HEALING & WHOLENESS

101 Scriptures & Guided Prayers for Day and Nighttime

Find Biblical Answers to Challenges of Body, Mind & Spirit.

A Similar Sister

Greensboro, NC 27401

God's Word for Healing and Wholeness

Published by Ellisean House Publishers
Greensboro, NC 27401

Cover art and book design by Richell Balansag

Ellisean House Publishers
Greensboro, NC 27401
www.elliseanhouse.com

Dedication

This book is lovingly dedicated to my Lord and Savior, Jesus, the Anointed Christ. You chose me when I was five years old to be Your own child. Through belief and unbelief, through joy and rage, You have never deserted me nor forgotten me…even when I deserted and forgot You.

What a mighty God You are!

This book is for You, Jesus.

With all my heart.

Disclaimer

Health challenges can be so difficult, and I have faith for your restoration to health and wholeness. I speak a breakthrough for you and pray for your complete healing. As you and I stand in faith, believing for your return to health and wholeness, be sure to practice both wisdom *and* faith.

Consult a qualified medical provider or healthcare professional. They will have opinions to offer regarding your health condition. You can discuss any concerns you have with them to make an informed decision. Please do not stop taking your medications nor disregard professional medical instructions.

Different people will have different results, as we are all made uniquely. I am standing with you in belief and prayer that God's Word and His promises are for you today *and* tomorrow. This includes healing that comes from the medical professions, prayer warriors, and elders of the church.

I would like to hear from you with any of your praise reports or prayer requests. You can reach me at:

similarsister@elliseanhouse.com

Thank you for purchasing Healing and Wholeness!

In gratitude, I want to send you a free gift. An e-book telling my backstory. Since I use a pen name for publishing, this will give you a little about me, my journey, and how I came to write this book.

Also, I would like to send you a beautiful personalized graphic, suitable for framing with the scripture of your choosing from the 101 choices in the book.

Send the scripture from the book you want. I will email a high-quality scripture picture back to you for printing. It is my hope this will be a faith builder for you or a friend and a reminder of God's love and power.

Additionally, as a bonus, I will include for you a bookmarks page in the same format with 5 of my favorite healing scriptures. You can have them laminated and give them away as gifts. A nice little keepsake for remembering God's living Word.

Finally, I would like to send you a recording of all these scriptures in my own voice. It is my hope that these scriptures will bring you comfort in wherever you find yourself and in whatever need you have. I received one such recording, about 30 years ago, back in the days of cassette tapes. It was a very bad recording, barely audible, but the Word of God shone through. I could not stop playing it. The living Word was so able to heal and save me, so I want to give you the same.

Always know that when you share your email with me it is a sacred trust and that it is never sold, rented or shared in any manner. Your confidentiality is assured.

Enjoy these gifts, with my love in the Lord.

Just drop me an email at similarsister@elliseanhouse.com

Contents

Introduction xiii
Chapter 1: My Profession of Faith 1
Chapter 2: Faith 3
Chapter 3: What is Healing? 8
Chapter 4: The Word and the Guided Prayer 12

PART 1

1. Hebrews 4:12 BSB 14
2. Isaiah 26:3 KJV 16
3. Matthew 9:29-30a BSB 18
4. Luke 11:19 NIV 20
5. 1 John 5:13-14 BSB 22
6. Matthew 4:23 NLT 24
7. Hebrews 12:2 BSB 26
8. Proverbs 16:24 BSB 28
9. John 8:12 NLT 30
10. Jeremiah 33:3 NASB 32
11. Luke 6:19 KJV 34
12. 1 John 3:22 NLT 36
13. Mark 3:9-11 BSB 38
14. Psalms 107:20 BSB 40
15. Job 33:28 NIV 42
16. Mark 5:26 NASB 44
17. 1 Kings 17:23 KJV 46
18. Galatians 5:1 NIV 48
19. Matthew 7:7 KJV 50
20. John 8:12 NLT 52
21. Galatians 2:19-21 AMP 54
22. Hosea 6:1 KJV 56

23. Proverbs 3:5-8 AMP 58
24. Psalms 118: 4-6 BSB 60
25. Isaiah 25:8 KJV 62
Chapter 5: The Word and the Guided Prayer 64

PART 2

26. Revelation 12:11 KJV 66
27. James 1:17 NLT 68
28. Daniel 2:22 NASB 70
29. PSALMS 1:1-3 NASB 72
30. Romans 8:12 KJV 74
31. Psalms 23:1-3 NIV 76
32. Ephesians 3:14-16 NIV 78
33. Acts 10:38 NLT 80
34. Matthew 4:23 BSB 82
35. Isaiah 38:18-20 NIV 84
36. Ezekiel 37:14 KJV 86
37. Matthew 8:2-3 BSB 88
38. Mark 2:4-11 BSB 90
39. 2 Peter 3:9 AMP 92
40. Romans 8:11 NIV 94
41. Proverbs 17:22 NLT 96
42. Matthew 10:8 NIV 98
43. Jonah 2:8-9 BSB 100
44. Isaiah 19:22 NIV 102
45. Matthew 6:34 AMP 104
46. Revelation 21:4 KJV 106
47. 1 Kings 8:37-39 KJV 108
48. Isaiah 53:4 NASB 110
49. Luke 4:40-41 NLT 112
Chapter 6: The Word and the Guided Prayer 114

PART 3

50. 2 Chronicles 16:9 NASB 116
51. Matthew 9:20-22 BSB 118
52. Psalm 3:1b-3 BSB 120
53. Jeremiah 17:14 NLT 122
54. Joel 3:10 KJV 124

55. Mark 5:40-42a BSB 126
56. Malachi 4:2 AMP 128
57. Jeremiah 33:6 KJV 130
58. Luke 15:4 NLT 132
59. Psalms 42:11 KJV 134
60. Proverbs 4:20-23 NASB 136
61. Luke 7:2-10 NIV 138
62. Isaiah 35:3-7 NIV 140
63. Jeremiah 30:16 KJV 142
64. Ezekiel 34:16a NASB 144
65. Matthew 14:35-36 NASB 146
66. Proverbs 15:4 KJV 148
67. Isaiah 53:4-5 BSB 150
68. Mark 3:9A NLT 152
69. Numbers 23:19 NLT 154
70. Deuteronomy 7:14-15a KJV 156
71. Matthew 15:22-29 BSB 158
72. 2 Kings 4:27-34 BSB 160
73. 2 Chronicles 6:14 NLT 162
74. Proverbs 3:1-2 KJV 164
Chapter 7: The Word and the Guided Prayer 166

PART 4

75. Matthew 11:29 NASB 168
76. Isaiah 58:8 KJV 170
77. 1 Peter 2:24 NLT 172
78. Psalms 80:18-19 BSB 174
79. 1 Peter 5:5b-7 NLT 176
80. Psalm 88:1-2 NASB 178
81. Isaiah 33:2 KJV 180
82. Matthew 19:26 NLT 182
83. Mark 6:12-13 NASB 184
84. Acts 9:17-19 NIV 186
85. Luke 9:11 NLT 188
86. John 21:25 KJV 190
87. Exodus 15:2 KJV 192
88. Psalms 119:107 NASB 194

89. Isaiah 46:4 NIV 196
90. 1 Peter 5:8 NLT 198
91. Psalm 80:17-19 NASB 200
92. Matthew 12:22 NLT 202
93. Acts 9: 36-37, 40-42 NIV 204
94. Psalms 105:37 KJV 206
95. Exodus 14:13-14 BSB 208
96. Proverbs 18:14 NIV 210
97. James 4: 14-15 212
98. Revelations 22:1 NLT 214
99. Timothy 1:9-10 NIV 216
100. Psalm 91:15-16 BSB 218
101. Romans 8:38-39 AMP 220
Chapter 8: A Prayer for Salvation 222
Afterword 223

Introduction

Hello, everyone! Welcome!

Welcome to God's Word for HEALING & WHOLENESS! 101 Bible Scriptures for Day and Nighttime.

Grace, Peace, and Well-Being to you all in the Name of Jesus Christ, our Savior.

Are you looking for healing for yourself or someone you love? Well, this is a fantastic place to start.

Here you will find the real Word of God from the Bible. A Bible version is shown, and, on a rare occasion, I will paraphrase a word or phrase for brevity or clarity. All true meanings of the Word with the reference and version will be available to you for the refreshing of your body, mind, and spirit.

Today we come to celebrate the healing power of the Word of God. There is nothing like the Word of God, and that is what scripture tells us is sharper than any two-edged sword, able to divide soul from spirit. If He can divide a soul from a spirit, surely God is able to divide sickness from our body and mind. He can make us whole and, in turn, make us able to worship Him even more, giving Him glory in our healing.

In God's Word lies the answer to all of our sicknesses and diseases no matter if they are of the body, mind, or spirit. How wonderful that is! That's something we can get behind, right?

Why did I write this book?

First of all, I wrote it for all of us who need a healing touch from God. Yes, me too. I believe there is healing for everyone and that the Word of God is the way to that healing.

Secondly, I believe that when we humble ourselves in prayer and listen to God's Word instead of being caught up in overusing technology, streaming shows, social media, and the like, we can hear God better through the Holy Spirit. He promised that the Holy Spirit would guide us into all truth.

He will bring to our remembrance the words He has written for us to feed off of, be cleansed by, and be healed through the increasing of our faith. When we make known to Him what we want exactly, according to God's Word, we will have it. (John 16:23)

Thirdly, I want to provide us with the weapons of our warfare right at our fingertips. His Word is easily accessible all day and even all night if you choose to listen to it. You can hear the Word of God in this book twenty-four hours a day, listening, reading, and recalling it to your mind.

How the book is organized.

In this book, we use selah to indicate a time to stop, listen with the inner ear, and reflect, just as the psalmist did. We want to think, really stop and think, about the scripture. This is where the healing thoughts and faith come from because "faith comes by hearing, and hearing by the Word of God." (Romans 10:17)

Because of the trial we are facing, this book starts with Scripture to build up our faith and continues with more faith encouragement integrated with Scripture dealing with the Word that speaks about healing. Some scripture may not sound appropriate to a healing situation, but this is the purpose of the selah. It gives time for God to speak to you in your mind and heart through the Holy Spirit.

I will repeat various iterations from the different gospels. There is a reason they are repeated by the gospel writers. Besides it *is* the Good News that feeds us, frees us, and fosters healing through faith in the Word of God.

The prayer section is broken up into chapters. This makes sense in the narrative, but maybe not so much with the rest of the book, one might think. This is not because there is any particular order to the scriptures. It is just for the sake of finding things that you may want to read or listen to again. You can note the page and/or chapter in your journal for reference much more easily this way. A whole book without any breaks is daunting. I have had some experiences with Bible-based audiobooks and journals without any reference, and it is very difficult to use.

My friend reminds me to "write it down," when something significant happens while I am studying the Word and am sharing it with her. So, I remind you and encourage you to preserve the precious Words to bring comfort to you in your time of need. I find that Bible margins are not enough!

Listening to the companion Audible book will be beneficial since you will hear the Word of God and it can sink deep into your conscious and unconscious mind awake or asleep. The soothing music in the Audible version is a great way to wind down when you want to sleep but feel like you can't.

Regarding gender, I will be using the masculine or feminine pronouns as are used in the Word. We know that, in the Kingdom of God, there is no difference in importance[1]. We are all one in Christ.

---

[1] Galatians 3:28

What will we learn in this book?

We learn that when we pray, meditate on and hear the Word of God, We open the way to healing we ask for. This is because we must hear and ask as well as believe God's words are true yesterday, today, and forevermore.

We put the Word of God into action and listen to Him–really hear, meditate, and pray for healing. Our faith is built up because faith comes by hearing and hearing by the Word of God. Yes, I said this before, but it's worth hearing again.

In this book, our guided prayers will focus on the directives from the Father, Jesus Christ, and the Holy Spirit, straight from our scripture reading. Both the Old and New Testaments provide evidence of Jesus, His mission, and His desire for our healing.

CHAPTER ONE

My Profession of Faith

I believe in the Father, Son, and Holy Ghost as written in scripture.

I believe in the power of the Word of God with all my heart.

I believe that Jesus died to save us and make us well. (Isaiah 53)

I believe that by the cross we are cleansed forever, healed forever, and made forever whole by the Savior, Jesus Christ, the Son of God.

God's Word tells the whole story. He loves us unconditionally.

I believe that when we accept Jesus as our Lord, we become, in Jesus, the very righteousness of God. This means that when God looks at us, He sees Jesus and all the things that He did for us so that we are no longer condemned for any reason or sin.

If we sin later, the Word says we are to confess our sin and He will be faithful and righteous to forgive us of all sin. This is the cup of Communion's purpose. It reminds us that Jesus' blood was spilled for the forgiveness of our sins.

We have not because we ask not, Jesus says, so gently. There is no condemnation in Him (Romans 8:1). Knock, seek and find are our new prayer paths where we can walk in freedom, for it was for freedom that Christ set us free (Galatians 5:1). This is the purpose of the broken body of Christ that we remember during our Communion time.

All we have to do is hear it, really hear it. We need to hear it in our minds and our hearts so that faith is sealed within them. But even if we think we doubt or don't have faith, then that is what we ask for. (Oh Lord, increase our faith!)

I have seen God at work in my own life through His mighty Word. I praise Him for the ongoing transformation of His presence in me.

CHAPTER TWO

Faith

Can faith in God's Word bring about our healing? YES! Resoundingly, YES!

With faith, we can see miracles. We can see Jesus' grace and mercy at work in our lives if we have that grain of mustard seed faith[2]. He does not ask much. Just know, believe, think and speak that He can do what His Word says.

Faith is so important. Jesus says all things are possible to him (or her) who believes. Please know that for many of us it is difficult to focus on the healing virtue of God when we are in pain and fear.

It can be hard to believe God's Word when things are going badly. Sometimes it seems Jesus is not with us as He promised. These are truly trying times, indeed. This is the purpose of our guided prayers. We speak to the Lord when we want to think another way, or can't think on the good things (Philippians 4:8)

I encourage you to use this book to speak out the truth of God's Word about faith and healing. We build up our faith when it feels

---

[2] Luke 17:6

like our faith has run out. Our faith can grow because we feel the healing power of God's Word.

I also offer this remedy for unbelief in your life. Find a song, make the music in your heart. Give thanks to God for everything.

> *"...be filled with the Spirit. Speak to one another with psalms, hymns, and spiritual songs. Sing and make music in your hearts to the Lord, always giving thanks to God the Father for everything in the name of our Lord Jesus Christ." – Ephesians 5:19-20 BSB*

The more we listen, speak and study, the more our minds become softer to the Word of God. Our faith is built up, giving us more faith and the peace we long for. God's abundant grace once again guards our hearts and minds in Christ Jesus (Philippians 4:7).

It is almost always that faith is directly associated with miraculous healings by Jesus and the apostles. This can be the return of our faith in Jesus for us. If we have never trusted Jesus, we may find our needs may drive us to Him.

There are simple prayers to pray to give our lives to the Lord without condemnation for things past. The key here is no condemnation. Jesus said He did not come to judge the world, but to save it. We are truthful about our sins in front of a Holy God, but we don't stand in condemnation. He is glad to receive us and wants us in His kingdom. Repentance is real and necessary, but we come to repentance by the Holy Spirit, following Jesus, because he loved us first. We just can't do it in our own willpower or strength.

These prayers include the ABCs of faith—Ask for salvation, Believe Jesus is the Son of God, and Confess Jesus as your Lord and Savior. I have included a prayer in the last chapter for those hearts that are ready to receive His blessings and healing. Jesus says He is the Way, the Truth, and the Life. He refuses no one who comes to Him, no matter who you are, no matter what you have done, no matter what (John 5:24).

Although there is a prayer for you at the end of the book, you can pray any prayer where you Ask Jesus to be Lord of your life, Believe that He is Lord of all, The Son of the Father sent for our forgiveness and healing, and believe that you *are* forgiven of all your sins ("missing the target" is the translation of sin). Then you Confess that Jesus is Lord out loud. "Now this is eternal life: that they know you, the only true God, and Jesus Christ, whom you have sent." (John 17:3)

We are asking for health and wholeness so that we can have that precious life. The amazing part is that He promises that eternal life is included in His life no matter what. We have earthly life and eternal life through Jesus Christ.

It does not matter what kind of sickness or pain or disease you face, God has put all things under Jesus' feet and Jesus is the Word of God (John 10) and He has overcome the law of sin and death (Romans 8:2). This is very important to understand, so I will say it again. Jesus has overcome the law of sin and death.

In John 14 and 15, Jesus says some very similar and life-changing words. He talks about how He is one in the Father and then He says that He is in us and we are in Him. Can you close your eyes and experience His Word directly applied to us? Jesus is in us, and we are in Him, and He is in the Father–that makes us in the Father also. Not forgetting the Holy Spirit since he is the Spirit of the Lord.

In John 17, Jesus prays that the disciples and all who listen to them, (That would be us), will be "One in Us." The Father, Jesus, and the Holy Spirit as well as us are all in the same place at the same time! We, too, are in the Father. The Father is all goodness and loving-kindness. He is all-powerful and all-knowing. He is the Almighty. All things are possible with God (Matt 19:26).

We are in the Divine Godhead. We are in the cloud of glory. We sit at the right hand of the Father in Jesus. Our prayers and petitions are being brought right to the very throne of God. How could we not receive what we ask for? It is in His Son's name that we lay our request at the Sovereign Presence.

We know that Jesus wants our healing because in John 14, 15, and 16 He says exactly that. Ask whatever you want in His will and the Father will give it to you.

"Truly, truly I say to you, if you ask the Father for anything in My name, He will give it to you. Until now you have asked for nothing in My name; ask and you will receive, so that your joy may be made full." (John 16: 23b-24)

He promises to send the Holy Spirit to us to be with us to guide us into all truth and impart wisdom.

Selah.

Sometimes a particular scripture is so significant to us that it becomes "*rehma*,"[3] the inbreathed, living Word of God. It feels like that was the Word for you at that very moment. We go back to revisit it to ponder what God is powerfully saying to us.

In the paperback version, you will find space to record the thoughts and revelations you receive. This helps you to remember what the Holy Spirit was bringing to your understanding. I don't know about you, but while I remember the Scripture itself sometimes, I often forget its personal significance given at that very moment.

Jesus asked a blind man specifically what he wanted. He feels the same toward us, just as I pointed out above. Be straightforward

---

3 https://iblp.org/questions/what-rhema

and real. There is no need to get fancy with God. He knows what we are going to ask even before we say it.

Our love overflows and we give thanks for answers to our prayers, knowing that they have been heard and the answers are on their way. At the proper time, all righteousness will be fulfilled. God is working even up to this hour and so our patience must be at work, too.

As the final thought of the chapter, thankfulness is what I want to remind all of us to show. Showing gratitude in every little thing not only glorifies God, but it also reminds us to praise Him for the smallest of blessings. He owes us nothing and there is nothing we can give Him that He cannot provide for Himself. If we neglect to praise Him, the rocks will cry out and the trees of the field will clap their hands. How much more pleasing it will be when His children give Him the thanks and the glory for His grace toward us.

CHAPTER THREE

What is Healing?

One very important thing to bring up is what healing consists of exactly, and what it looks like. You might think of questions such as "how will I feel?" and "how will I know if I'm being healed?"

We really must consider any and all healing by whatever means, to be healing from God. Sometimes we want to discount doctors and medicine and other health practitioners and practices, but, my dear friend, this could be causing you to lose out on some of the greatest blessings you can have.

Selah

It could also cost you your life if you are anything like me. Let me share a personal story.

I was at a prayer meeting one night and I felt a twinge on my right side. I just shrugged it off as I do most little aches and pains. Well, it turned out not to be such a minor detail.

For three weeks I was in progressively increasing, terrible pain but did not seek medical help. We had no health insurance (this was before Obamacare), and I was sure I was just passing some gallstones.

Since I have had gallstones fall out before without any problems, I didn't worry about it too much. My step Mom suggested taking antacid calcium tablets. You know, those fruity chewable ones? So, there I am, eating tablets and not much else, and still getting sicker and sicker.

My daughter told me later that my skin was gray-tinged. I always think of Mr. Gray, as medical students call their practice cadavers.

I had always been afraid of dying. I had always been afraid of operations. But God gave me a supernatural experience that showed me that no matter how things were, all would be okay, with or without me.

Finally, this old hardhead here went to the emergency room but by then I had no more fear of dying. I had been praying for a miracle you see, like maybe a Bolt from the Blue? Or something along those lines, certainly not the dreaded hospital. Ha! Little did I know that my appendix had burst three weeks earlier at that prayer meeting.

Well, as God would have it, it turned out that the hospital, when I got there, didn't move very quickly. It took another whole day before they decided they had to operate. One minute I am telling the pastor on the phone "Oh, it must be nothing because no one is in any hurry." No sooner did that come out of my mouth when a male nurse was scurrying up to my bed and rolling me into surgery. Surprise!

It turned out to be a very serious surgery, and I lost half of my colon. During the surgery, the doctor found a lump like a rock that looked like a tumor. So, he did a hemicolectomy and sent the lump off for a pathology report. No one said a word to me about all of this until one evening about a week later, when the surgeon came in to tell me the story.

You see, that rock was no tumor at all, but–wait for it–calcium from all the antacids I had taken! All that calcium kept me alive by God's suggestion through my step Mom. Those tablets were detoxing me after my appendix burst, binding all the poisons up in that little rock.

People would normally die three days after a burst appendix from sepsis (blood poisoning). I lived three weeks before I even found myself in the hospital! How miraculous! How great a healer our God is!

It was not my hoped-for Bolt from the Blue, but a miracle nonetheless, with God's hand through my medical team and His faithful hand right on me. It wasn't the fastest healing ever, but I am alive to tell you that even if things are dire, dearest friends, trust God. Healing can come in stages. Imagine the 30-, 60-, and 100-fold blessings Jesus spoke of (Matt 13:23).

I was saved by reading the Bible. Believe me when I say I have been saved from death more than five times. I was healed from a nervous breakdown. I have prayed the Word of God over others and seen them healed and forever set free from many things.

I am not writing this book because I have arrived, nor because I need no more healing. Neither is it because I'm some great preacher or faith healer. I am writing this book because I must. I just can't get away from it. The need to do this chases me down. The Lord will not take no for an answer.

In all earnestness, I am praying for you right now. At this very moment. We need healing and miracles in our midst right now more than ever as the day of the Lord's return draws near.

God's Word works wonders. There is no doubt about it. We do not doubt because we know His Word is true.

I encourage you to read the disclaimer at the beginning of the book. In no way is this book or anything therein to be considered medical advice, nor act as a substitute for seeking professional help.

I have nothing to offer you other than the Word of God. But that is enough. Follow wisdom, as it advises us in Proverbs, and get the help you need without fear. God will handle the rest.

So, we begin our journey through the Word to come before the Throne of God through Jesus Christ. We ask for mercy and grace in times of trouble, expecting to receive what we ask for according to God's will, and just as it says in God's Word. We look forward to God's promised healing. We sing songs of gratitude to our King who died that we might be free to receive the grace of His oft-repeated healing words in the Bible. Jesus' life can be considered a true reflection of the Father's desire to heal us. It is His grace and mercy that leads us to the faith we need to receive His divine health and wholeness.

CHAPTER 4

The Word and the Guided Prayer

Part 1

1. HEBREWS 4:12 BSB

For the word of God is living and active. Sharper than any double-edged sword, it pierces even to dividing soul and spirit, joints and marrow. It judges the thoughts and intentions of the heart.

Selah

Lord, Your Word is living and it's active. It's sharper than any sword. It pierces and divides my soul and body from every evil thing. I can't think of anyone or anything that could be more powerful working on my behalf.

I am set free.

Thank You for setting me free by the power of Your Word, since those are the thoughts and intentions of my heart. I seek after You to receive the blessings of faith in You. Thank You for protecting me from the evil one. Thank You for always watching over me and using the mighty weapons of Your warfare.

You really are not fooling around when it comes to my protection and I am so grateful. With all my heart... in Jesus' Name. Amen.

____

____

____

____

____

2. ISAIAH 26:3 KJV

THOU WILT KEEP HIM IN PERFECT PEACE, WHOSE MIND IS STAYED ON THEE: BECAUSE HE TRUSTETH IN THEE.

Selah

Lord, thank You for Your perfect peace as my mind stays focused on You. Oh, Jesus, You are the gentle and meek Prince of Peace. You guard my heart and mind with Your love for me. It is hard to comprehend that kind of love.

I have never really had that kind of love before meeting You. Today I open my heart to Your peace and love because I do trust in you. Through Your Holy Spirit I know I can do all things, even wait for and expect my healing that comes with the angels, sent from Your throne with healing in their wings.

Thank you for healing every part of me, now and for all time. I trust in You with all my heart.

In Jesus' name, Amen.

3. MATTHEW 9:29–30A BSB

THEN HE TOUCHED THEIR EYES AND SAID, "ACCORDING TO YOUR FAITH WILL IT BE DONE TO YOU." AND THEIR EYES WERE OPENED.

Selah

Lord, please also touch me so that by faith Your healing may be done for me. I know that when You touched those blind men, You, through the cross, touched me too, because You are no respecter of persons.

Your healing is for everyone who believes You came from God and are God. I know this work is done through Your death at the cross, so I believe that You are healing me. By Your stripes, I am healed.

Thank You for helping me and strengthening my faith in You, by the power of the Holy Spirit, now and from this day forward.

In Jesus Christ's name, Amen.

4. LUKE 11:19 NIV

"AND SO I TELL YOU, KEEP ON ASKING, AND YOU WILL RECEIVE WHAT YOU ASK FOR. KEEP ON SEEKING, AND YOU WILL FIND. KEEP ON KNOCKING, AND THE DOOR WILL BE OPENED TO YOU.

Selah

Lord of all, thank You for not getting tired of me coming to You with healing requests. I am grateful for the reminder to keep on asking and to keep on seeking and to keep on knocking on Your door.

Thank You for always watching for the littlest show of faith on my part to bless me. I pray for my faith to grow by believing Your Word and by the power of the Holy Spirit.

Thank You for healing me. Thank You for continually watching over me even as Your healing continues. Thank You for putting my faith to work in believing Your words are true.

I pray in Your name, Jesus. Amen.

5. 1 JOHN 5:13–14 BSB

I have written these things to you who believe in the name of the Son of God, so that you may know that you have eternal life. And this is the confidence that we have before Him: If we ask anything according to His will, He hears us. And if we know that He hears us in whatever we ask, we know that we already possess what we have asked of Him.

Selah

Lord, as John writes, I believe that I have eternal life through believing in You, the Son of God and Your holy name. Thank You, Lord, for the confidence I have in standing before You.

Your Word says If I ask You anything according to Your will, You hear me. I know Your will for me is healing because You suffered and died in my place. You healed thousands on this earth while you walked with us. I know this is Your true will because from the beginning to the end of the Bible You tell me about Your desire and promise to heal me.

Thank You for healing me by the power of Your suffering and death, oh, Sinless Lamb. I thank You always and pray in Your name, Lord Jesus. Amen.

6. MATTHEW 4:23 NLT

JESUS TRAVELED THROUGHOUT THE REGION OF GALILEE, TEACHING IN THE SYNAGOGUES AND ANNOUNCING THE GOOD NEWS ABOUT THE KINGDOM. AND HE HEALED EVERY KIND OF DISEASE AND ILLNESS.

Selah

Thank You, Father, for sending Jesus to walk this earth as a man, but yet sinless. I listen to the Good News about the kingdom, that Jesus is the Son of God and God the Son who died that I might live through the Living God.

I thank You for such lovingkindness and healing. His selflessness on this earth was unparalleled. Every day He preached the good news of the Kingdom of Heaven on earth. Every day He healed the sick. Every day He spoke what He heard directly from You. Your compassion toward us, as revealed by Jesus is without compare.

By Your Spirit, I pray that I, too, may hear directly from You through Your Word and Your whisperings to my soul and spirit. I pray that I obey Your Word and do what is right in Your sight, even as Jesus, my model, and Savior did. Through the power you gave us in the Holy Spirit, I give You all glory, honor, and blessing. Thank You for sending Jesus. Thank You for all Your many blessings. Thank You for Your everlasting love.

I pray in Jesus' name. Amen.

7. HEBREWS 12:2 BSB

LOOKING ONLY AT JESUS, THE ORIGINATOR AND PERFECTER OF THE FAITH, WHO FOR THE JOY SET BEFORE HIM ENDURED THE CROSS, DESPISING THE SHAME, AND HAS SAT DOWN AT THE RIGHT HAND OF THE THRONE OF GOD.

Selah

Jesus, I look only at You. You are the author and perfecter of my faith.

You endured the cross so that You would overcome death and the grave. How I long to always keep my eyes on You. By Your Holy Spirit help me not waver, falter or be so distracted that I forget to keep looking!

I am so glad my failings are nothing at all to You, and that You have made provision for the healing of everyone. Even though I often feel underserving or less worthy than others, that "everyone" includes me, too.

Thank You, Lord, that You despised the shame of the cross and now You sit at the right hand of the Father to intercede for me.

I pray in the name of Jesus. Amen.

8. PROVERBS 16:24 BSB

PLEASANT WORDS ARE A HONEYCOMB, SWEET TO THE SOUL, AND HEALING TO THE BONES.

Selah

Father, thank You for Your pleasant words. You have made them so sweet! They are life and healing to me. You care for my soul and spirit as You care for my body. Hallelujah!

There is never a time when You forget this Word You spoke so long ago. I pray You to ignite these words in my heart and mind now, by the Power of Your Spirit, so that I may benefit even more from this reading.

I ask for healing and wholeness for my soul and bones, Lord, knowing that You hear me by the name of Jesus.

In Jesus's name, I pray. Amen.

9. JOHN 8:12 NLT

JESUS SPOKE TO THE PEOPLE ONCE MORE AND SAID, "I AM THE LIGHT OF THE WORLD. IF YOU FOLLOW ME, YOU WON'T HAVE TO WALK IN DARKNESS, BECAUSE YOU WILL HAVE THE LIGHT THAT LEADS TO LIFE."

Selah

Oh, glorious Light of the world! How I love You because You first loved me! Oh, how I praise You! How I look for You every day in my life, in my heart, in my spirit, and in my mind!

You came to die that I might live. There is none like You, oh, Lord. Your death and resurrection make all the difference. How You could endure such suffering is not something I understand. Still, I hope I can grab onto the faith that You died for me.

I thank You that I don't walk in darkness because You are the light, Lord, that leads me to eternal life. I don't think I remember about darkness very much, but it does try to sneak up and try to grab me when I don't keep my eyes on You.

Thank You, Holy Spirit, for keeping me always walking in the light of Jesus.

I pray in Jesus' name. Amen.

10. JEREMIAH 33:3 NASB

'Call to Me and I will answer you, and I will tell you great and mighty things, which you do not know.'

Selah

Father, Abba (Daddy)! I call to You! Oh Lord, show me great and mighty things which I do not know.

Thank You for Your miracles, Lord. I humble myself before You in Your righteousness that is in Jesus. I long to know the mysteries of Your healing in me, but I know You reveal these things in Your own time, and in Your own way.

Thank you for the honor of knowing Your thoughts as You have revealed them in Your Word. Thank You for counting me as worthy of revelation from the Holy Spirit.

I pray that my life is a testimony of the great and incomparable glory of God. And, Lord, may Your unsurpassed revelation be shown in my life to those who need to hear the revelation of You as the God Who Heals, Our Jehovah Jireh.

I pray in the mighty name of Jesus. Amen.

11. LUKE 6:19 KJV

AND THE WHOLE MULTITUDE SOUGHT TO TOUCH HIM: FOR THERE WENT VIRTUE OUT OF HIM, AND HEALED THEM ALL.

Selah

Lord, My God! I, too, reach out to touch You and receive Your healing virtue. Thank You for letting me touch You for my healing. Thank You, Jesus, for suffering in my place, so that I can receive healing by Your grace and mercy, now and forever. Your grace is never-ending because in Christ I am Your righteousness.

I am not worthy of Your healing virtue on my own merits, but You purchased my healing on the cross. You have made me the righteousness of God in Jesus Christ. That's YOUR righteousness, Father. All purity and holiness!

Thank You, Lord. And in Your name Jesus, I pray. Amen

12. 1 JOHN 3:22 NLT

AND WE WILL RECEIVE FROM HIM WHATEVER WE ASK BECAUSE WE OBEY HIM AND DO THE THINGS THAT PLEASE HIM.

Selah

Thank You, Lord, for I receive whatever I ask for because I desire to obey You and do the things that please You. I know that believing in Jesus is the thing You desire most from me. And I thank You for sending Your only Son to save me.

I want to keep Your commandments by the power of the Holy Spirit, because in my strength alone, I cannot, especially now that I feel weakened. Still, I know that You have Your hand on me to care for me always.

If we make a mistake, You are faithful and just to forgive us from all unrighteousness, because in Christ, I am the righteousness of God. In Christ, I am free! In Christ, I have all my prayers answered just as it says here in Your Word.

In Jesus's name, I pray. Amen.

13. MARK 3:9–11 BSB

Jesus asked His disciples to have a boat ready for Him so that the crowd would not crush Him. For He had healed so many that all who had diseases were pressing forward to touch Him. And when the unclean spirits saw Him, they fell down before Him and cried out, "You are the Son of God!"

Selah

Dear Father, even the evil demons knew You sent Your Son Jesus to be the agent of our healing, and they forced the possessed to bow down before you.

How much more do I want to bow before the throne of God to acknowledge Jesus, the Holy One of Israel. I bow my heart before You Jesus, to thank You for dying so that I might live.

I proclaim that You, Jesus, are the Son of God and the Son of Man and that You are now, in Your glorified body, waiting for me.

I thank You, Lord and in Your name, I pray. Amen.

14. PSALMS 107:20 BSB

He healed them with his command and saved them from the grave.

Selah

Oh, Lord, it is Your command that saves me from the grave. Thank You for the victory over the grave that Jesus purchased with His body and blood.

Thank You for victory over the law of sin and death, Jesus. You know me from the inside out and nothing is hidden from You.

Thank You for providing for me before now, during the present, and in the future for how I feel and how I live. There is no love like Yours, Father.

In Jesus' name, Amen.

15. JOB 33:28 NIV

God has delivered me from going down to the pit, and I shall live to enjoy the light of life.

Selah

Yes! Hooray, God! You have delivered me from the pit. Your Word says right here that I shall live to enjoy the light of life. I receive it from You, Jesus.

Job knew all about that suffering that makes us doubt You and start to question You about Your motives.

When his suffering was done, You showed Job and me that You are beyond understanding. Your thoughts are as far as the east is from the west. You are the great Creator and there was no one to watch or give You directions at the foundation of the world. Thank You for Your mighty deeds.

There is no one like You and I am so grateful for the opportunities You give me to live my life to the fullest possibilities now and in the future.

In Jesus' name, Amen.

____

____

____

____

16. MARK 5:26 NASB

And wherever He entered villages, or cities, or a countryside, they were laying the sick in the marketplaces and imploring Him that they might just touch the fringe of His cloak; and all who touched it were being healed.

Selah

Lord, in that day people could physically touch You for Your gracious (undeserved) healing. Lord, since there is no separation in time or space. I, too, reach out my hand now to touch You. I, too, just reach out in my spirit, to touch You. I believe Your healing is for me today.

I believe that Your health and wholeness living in You is now also living in me. Please know that I am so filled with thanksgiving.

I'm looking forward to practicing Your presence in my life always, and at all times.

In Jesus' name, Amen.

17. 1 KINGS 17:23 KJV

And Elijah took the child, and brought him down out of the chamber into the house, and delivered him unto his mother: and Elijah said, See, thy son liveth.

Selah

Even in the days of old, Lord, were working miracles. You have compassion on Your people whose heart is toward You. Lord, I give my heart to You, so that I, too, may be brought back from death to life.

It is Your promise that, if I ask, the Father will give it to me in Your name. So, I ask for a life overflowing with Your grace and mercy. I ask for my specific needs of healing and wholeness to be met.

I believe that You will do this because You always fulfill Your word. You are not a man that You lie. There is no reason to doubt or lack faith for my healing when so great a miracle was performed before the coming of Jesus. Now that He has died for me, I have access to all Your blessings.

Thank You in Jesus' name. Amen.

18. GALATIANS 5:1 NIV

It is for freedom that Christ has set us free. Stand firm, then, and do not let yourselves be burdened again by a yoke of slavery.

Selah

Marvelous Lord, how glorious it is that it was for freedom that You set me free.

No longer am I a slave in bondage to any sickness, pain, disease, or any thoughts of such things. I am free and no longer a slave to any except Christ.

Oh, thank You Jesus for suffering so that I might be healed and live. Thank You for Your freedom. I could shout it out. It is so powerful. Your word is life and health to me, Lord. Thank You.

In faith, these prayers can heal me. You never forget me in Your Word. How I love You since You have an everlasting love for me. Thank You for making me well by faith. What a loving and merciful God I serve! There is no one like You, Lord.

In Jesus' name, I pray. Amen.

19. MATTHEW 7:7 KJV

ASK, AND IT WILL BE GIVEN TO YOU; SEEK, AND YOU WILL FIND; KNOCK, AND IT WILL BE OPENED TO YOU.

Selah

How generous You are, oh, Lord. I can ask and it will be given. I can seek and I will find and I can knock and You will open the door. Your Holy Spirit leads me there.

No matter how I approach You, I will have the healing You bought and paid for with Your body and blood. I believe You will reveal to me the mysteries of God by Your Holy Spirit, so that I may be strong and faithful.

I so look forward to and believe I will see You when I ask, seek, and knock.

In Your name, Jesus, I pray. Amen.

20. JOHN 8:12 NLT

Jesus spoke to the people once more and said, "I am the light of the world. If you follow me, you won't have to walk in darkness, because you will have the light that leads to life."

Selah

Oh, glorious Light of the world! How I love You. Oh, how I praise You. How I look for You every day in my life, in my heart, spirit, and in my mind.

I love You because You loved me first. You came to die that I might live. There is none like You, oh, Lord.

I thank You that I don't walk in darkness because You are the light, Lord, that leads me to eternal life. I don't think I have thought about darkness, but it does try to sneak up and try to grab me when I don't keep my eyes on You.

Thank You, Holy Spirit, for keeping me always walking in the light of Jesus. I pray in Jesus' name. Amen.

21. GALATIANS 2:19–21 AMP

For through the Law, I died to the Law and its demands on me [because salvation is provided through the death and resurrection of Christ], so that I might [from now on] live to God. I have been crucified with Christ [that is, in Him, I have shared His crucifixion]; it is no longer I who live, but Christ lives in me. The life I now live in the body I live by faith [by adhering to, relying on, and completely trusting] in the Son of God, who loved me and gave Himself up for me. I do not ignore or nullify the [gracious gift of the] grace of God [His amazing, unmerited favor], for if righteousness comes through [observing] the Law, then Christ died needlessly. [His suffering and death would have had no purpose whatsoever.]

Selah

Lord, doing away with the Law was not Your plan, was it? It is more that You fulfilled every single one of those laws in Jesus Christ, by His death and resurrection. Thank You that I no longer live under the Law, but am free in Your righteousness in Christ Jesus.

Thank You that I can celebrate the cross as my promise of eternal life. Thank You that I can rejoice that the Law is fulfilled. The Law has no further hold on me.

Freedom is such a big thing, it's hard to really comprehend, but I make a conscious effort to understand by the leading of the Holy Spirit.

Thank You for making me Your righteousness in Jesus. I pray in the mighty name of Jesus. Amen

22. HOSEA 6:1 KJV

Come, let us return to the Lord. For He has torn us to pieces, but He will heal us; He has wounded us, but He will bind up our wounds. After two days He will revive us; on the third day He will raise us up, that we may live in His presence.

Selah

Lord, You are a merciful God. Israel was sinning with false idols and forgot about You and Your love for Your people. Yet, even then You healed them. How much more now that Jesus has come do You pour out Your healing virtue on Your very own blood-bought children.

I am amazed that You use "us" to refer to You *and* Jesus, over 400 years before His birth. Over 400 years until Jesus refers to the unity of the apostles and their followers as being "in Us."

Thank You for never giving up on me, Lord, even when I went my own way. Thank You for this beautiful picture of the crucifixion and resurrection of Jesus. On our behalf, You tore Him, then bandaged Him. You revived Him and raised Him. Even so, I am raised in the newness of life in Jesus.

I thank You, Lord God. In Jesus' name. Amen

23. PROVERBS 3:5-8 AMP

Trust in and rely confidently on the Lord with all Your heart, and do not rely on Your own insight or understanding. In all your ways, know and acknowledge and recognize Him, and He will make your paths straight and smooth [removing obstacles that block your way].

Do not be wise in your own eyes; Fear the Lord [with reverent awe and obedience] and turn [entirely] away from evil.

It will be health to your body [your marrow, your nerves, your sinews, your muscles—all your inner parts] and refreshment (physical well-being) to your bones.

Selah

Dearest Lord, I come to lean on You, to trust You with all my heart. Because You say so, I won't trust in my own understanding of things. I will not count myself wise in my own eyes. I will keep my eyes fixed on You.

Thank You for always making my paths straight so that I do not stumble in my faith. Still, I know that I can lay all things at Your feet to receive that refreshing feeling in my mind, spirit, and body. Thank You, Lord, for explaining these things to me. I will remember all this by the prompting of the Holy Spirit.

I pray in Your name, Jesus. Amen.

24. PSALMS 118: 4–6 BSB

Let those who fear the Lord say, "His loving devotion endures forever." In my distress, I called to the Lord, and He answered and set me free. The Lord is on my side; I will not be afraid. What can man do to me?

Selah

Lord, along with all others who lovingly fear You, I say, Your loving devotion endures forever. I do call on You in my distress. You answer me and set me free.

Since You are on my side, and I know You truly are, no one can do anything to me. I will be fearless in You. Your Holy Spirit guides me and keeps me close to You.

You said You would never leave nor forsake me and I thank You that when I call on You, You always come to help me.

In Your name, Jesus, I pray.

25. ISAIAH 25:8 KJV

He will swallow up death for all time, and the Lord GOD will wipe tears away from all faces, and He will remove the disgrace of His people from all the earth; For the LORD has spoken.

Selah

Removing our disgrace, Lord, is huge. Swallowing up death for all time is almost unfathomable. I can barely wrap my head around how big a work that is.

How tender and loving You are. You wipe my tears away. Oh, Jesus, how You suffered to make such a wonderful thing happen. I am humbled in the face of such tenderness. I am shaken to my core by Your never-ending love.

Thank You that death has no hold on me because of Your sacrifice. By Your stripes, I am healed. May Your name be glorified forever.

I pray in the mighty name of Jesus. Amen.

CHAPTER FIVE

The Word and the Guided Prayer

Part 2

26. REVELATION 12:11 KJV

AND THEY OVERCAME HIM BY THE BLOOD OF THE LAMB, AND BY THE WORD OF THEIR TESTIMONY, AND THEY LOVED NOT THEIR LIVES UNTO THE DEATH.

Selah

Lord, here we see those who love You so much that they overcame the enemy by Your blood, dear Lamb of God, and by the word of their testimony.

They even gave up their lives to You for the Kingdom's sake.

May I be brave in the face of suffering because I know You have heard me pray for my healing and You will give me health and wholeness by Your abundant grace. May my testimony be always to the greatness of my God.

I pray in Jesus' name. Amen.

27. JAMES 1:17 NLT

WHATEVER IS GOOD AND PERFECT IS A GIFT COMING DOWN TO US FROM GOD OUR FATHER, WHO CREATED ALL THE LIGHTS IN THE HEAVENS. HE NEVER CHANGES OR CASTS A SHIFTING SHADOW.

Selah

How kind and wonderful You are dear Lord, our Father. I rejoice to know that all good and perfect things that come to me from You are Your gifts to me.

I gladly receive the gift of vibrant health and well-being. To meditate on You, creating the heavenly lights, is awesome. You are the all-knowing, all-seeing God.

I praise You that You never change nor do You ever cast shadows that leave me in darkness when I approach You.

I pray in the name of the Lord, Jesus Christ. Amen.

28. DANIEL 2:22 NASB

It is He who reveals the profound and hidden things; He knows what is in the darkness, and the light dwells with Him.

Selah

Oh Lord, I praise You that it is You who reveals the profound and hidden things. No one else has this kind of knowledge.

Lord, I thank You that You know what is in the darkness, and then You can, and do, reveal things to me. You even reveal things I can't begin to imagine. Sometimes the things I have been seeking for a long time, You in Your perfect timing reveal this truth hidden in the darkness.

Lord, light dwells with You. In the Book of John, You said Jesus is the Light, so I embrace You in all of Your manifestations. You are holy, almighty, all-knowing, and all-blessing.

Thank You that I will never walk in darkness as long as I am with You.

I pray in Jesus' name. Amen.

29. PSALMS 1:1–3 NASB

Blessed is the person who does not walk in the counsel of the wicked, nor stand in the path of sinners, nor sit in the seat of scoffers! But His delight is in the Law of the Lord, and in His Law, he meditates day and night. He will be like a tree planted by streams of water, which yields its fruit in its season, and its leaf does not wither; And in whatever he does, he prospers.

Selah

Lord, let me not listen to the advice of those who do not live by Your precepts unless the Holy Spirit deems it appropriate.

I avoid the wicked. I seek the company of Your people who build me up and do not tear me down. My delight is in Your word. I meditate on it day and night.

Thank You for telling me that I am like a tree planted by refreshing streams of water. Thank You that I will yield Your fruit in season and I will not wither up.

I receive this as healing for my mind, body, and spirit for the rest of my life. I glorify You for all Your mighty deeds.

I pray in the mighty name of Jesus. Amen.

30. ROMANS 8:12 KJV

For the law of the Spirit of life in Christ Jesus has made me free from the law of sin and death.

Selah

Oh God, I praise You for the Spirit of life in Christ Jesus.

You have set me free from the law of sin and death. You have set me free! Thank You, Lord, for Your free healing. You don't change your mind. I am free forever.

I have not ever realized that I have been in bondage because I believe in you. Still, I have tried to follow laws and traditions instead of just following You!

What grace and freedom are available to change my beliefs and now allow me to have real faith in You, unencumbered with man's ways and thoughts about who You might be.

Oh, thank You so much. In Jesus' name, Amen.

31. PSALMS 23:1–3 NIV

The Lord is my shepherd, I lack nothing. He makes me lie down in green pastures, He leads me beside quiet waters, He refreshes my soul. He guides me along the right paths for his name's sake.

Selah

Father, thank You for being my shepherd. Thank You that I lack for nothing. I have everything in You.

You bring me into the quiet places in the middle of the noise and confusion of everyday life. You are refreshing me right now! I receive Your green pastures, sweet, clean water, and Your precious guidance.

I can't do anything to change things in my own strength, so thank You for always being there to get me through.

In Jesus' name, I pray, Amen.

32. EPHESIANS 3:14–16 NIV

For this reason, I bow my knees before the Father, from whom every family in heaven and on earth derives its name, that He would grant you, according to the riches of His glory, to be strengthened with power through His Spirit in your inner man.

Selah

Oh, Father, please do strengthen me in my inner being. I am weak and needy without Your eternal grace. I deserve no such favor, but I am so truly grateful for it.

You grant such mercies and unmerited acts of kindness and love toward me. I know that it is from within that health flows by Your power and Holy Spirit. I look for Your presence inside me.

Your grace is more than I deserve, but Your love acts on my behalf, warding off my evil enemies at all times. Holy Spirit.

Thank You for guiding me into all truth. I thank You for Your wisdom in showing me the path I need to follow now. And I thank You that You never leave me or forsake me, even in my time of weakness.

In Jesus' name, Amen.

33. ACTS 10:38 NLT

And you know that God anointed Jesus of Nazareth with the Holy Spirit, and with power. Then Jesus went around doing good and healing all who were oppressed by the devil, for God was with him.

Selah

Oh, dear Lord, pour out Your Holy Spirit and power on me now. I need Your healing and freedom from oppression.

Jesus, I believe that You still go around doing good and healing all who need You by the power of Your Spirit, so, I am ready to receive You now.

Thank You for sending Your Holy Spirit to me now, and healing my every need in body, mind, and spirit. Just as Jesus did then, He does now.

Thank You, Lord, that it is always Your intention to continue Your healing into my future also.

In Jesus' name, Amen.

34. MATTHEW 4:23 BSB

JESUS WENT THROUGHOUT GALILEE, TEACHING IN THEIR SYNAGOGUES, PREACHING THE GOSPEL OF THE KINGDOM, AND HEALING EVERY DISEASE AND SICKNESS AMONG THE PEOPLE.

Selah

God, thank You that You send Jesus out openly into the world. He did not only tell of the Good News, He showed it with all the healings and miracles.

I thank You today that I, too, have the Good News that Jesus came to free the world from sin and death. Thank You for healing me, now and always. Thank you for the freedom that You give me, *Grace*, unmerited, unearned, and unfathomable!

Thank You for my own miracle of Your work in my life. Thank You for changing me into Your image, and making me whole and well.

In Jesus' name, Amen.

35. ISAIAH 38:18-20 NIV

For the grave cannot praise you, death cannot sing your praise; those who go down to the pit cannot hope for your faithfulness. The living, the living—they praise you, as I am doing today; parents tell their children about your faithfulness. The Lord will save me, and we will sing with stringed instruments all the days of our lives in the temple of the Lord...

Selah

Oh, Lord, how You show mercy to those who have followed Your ways as King Hezekiah did here. He had a septic boil that would not heal and his death was imminent. When Your prophet Isaiah came and heard from You, he put a mustard poultice on it, and it healed. No wonder Hezekiah was praising You. Divinely directed medicine healed him in time to save his life.

When I have to take medicine or go through a procedure, let me be guided by Your Holy Spirit even as Isaiah was to perform Your will. Let me receive it as the King did. I will obey Your directions and trust You to take over. Let me know wisdom and have faith to do the right thing.

I sing praises of joy for Your goodness. I pray in Jesus' name. Amen.

36. EZEKIEL 37:14 KJV

I SHALL PUT MY SPIRIT IN YOU, AND YE SHALL LIVE, AND I SHALL PLACE YOU IN YOUR OWN LAND: THEN SHALL YE KNOW THAT I THE LORD HAVE SPOKEN IT, AND PERFORMED IT, SAITH THE LORD.

Selah

Thank You, Lord, for Your Holy Spirit, to lead and guide me in my journey to wholeness.

You said You will always be with me and I believe it. You have spoken it. You have performed it. You have said it is done.

So be it in my mind and heart to further my healing and keep my mind always focused on You.

All glory to You, my God!

In Jesus' name, Amen.

37. MATTHEW 8:2-3 BSB

AND A LEPER CAME TO HIM AND BOWED DOWN BEFORE HIM, AND SAID, "LORD, IF YOU ARE WILLING, YOU CAN MAKE ME CLEAN." JESUS STRETCHED OUT HIS HAND AND TOUCHED HIM, SAYING, "I AM WILLING; BE CLEANSED." AND IMMEDIATELY HIS LEPROSY WAS CLEANSED.

Selah

Oh, my dearest Friend, I praise You for Your compassion. "If You are willing..." Thank You for always being willing to heal. You placed no conditions for cleansing this leper.

Oh Lord, thank You. I praise You for looking on my lowly state and not turning away, even as You did not turn from the leper's uncleanness and highly contagious disease.

My sickness, although it may want to make others turn from me, does not scare You nor cause You to turn from me. I sing Hallelujah! Not in some weird way, but from my heart, Hallelujah!

Cleanse, me Lord. Heal me, my King. I believe in You. I believe You are willing to heal me fully.

I thank You and I praise You.

In Your name, Jesus. Amen.

38. MARK 2:4–11 BSB

Then a paralytic was brought to Him, carried by four men Since they were unable to get to Jesus through the crowd, they uncovered the roof above Him, made an opening, and lowered the paralytic on his mat. When Jesus saw their faith, He said to the paralytic, "Son, your sins are forgiven." But some of the scribes were sitting there and thinking in their hearts, "Why does this man speak like this? He is blaspheming! Who can forgive sins but God alone?"

At once Jesus knew in His spirit that they were thinking this way within themselves. "Why are you thinking these things in your hearts?" He asked. "Which is easier: to say to a paralytic, 'Your sins are forgiven,' or to say, 'Get up, pick up your mat, and walk'? But so that you may know that the Son of Man has authority on earth to forgive sins..." He said to the paralytic, "I tell you, get up, pick up your mat, and go home." And immediately the man got up, picked up his mat, and walked out in front of them all. As a result, they were all astounded and glorified God, saying, "We have never seen anything like this!"

Selah

What a commotion this must have caused to see a paralyzed man being lowered down in such a crowd. Jesus, for You to say his sins were forgiven must have been a blessing and a disappointment to that man at the same time, since he came to be healed.

What the paralytic may not have realized was that it was because he stepped over the line and missed the mark in his lifestyle, that it was sin that caused his illness. He didn't have Jesus in his life. Jesus, You hadn't died for him yet. He didn't have access before to the forgiveness Jesus offered him right then and there.

Sometimes I feel my lifestyle needs adjusting. I know I do not stand condemned because I am the righteousness of God in Jesus Christ. Guilt has no part in me because of my confession. I still need to make some changes. Lord, help me make my body a temple of the Holy Spirit. Thank You, for being Lord over my sickness, pain, and disease. All praise to You for hearing my confession and my cry.

In Jesus' name, I pray. Amen.

39. 2 PETER 3:9 AMP

THE LORD DOES NOT DELAY [AS THOUGH HE WERE UNABLE TO ACT] AND IS NOT SLOW ABOUT HIS PROMISE, AS SOME COUNT SLOWNESS, BUT IS [EXTRAORDINARILY] PATIENT TOWARD YOU, NOT WISHING FOR ANY TO PERISH BUT FOR ALL TO COME TO REPENTANCE.

Selah

Yes, Lord. It's true. I often think You aren't working fast enough on my behalf, or that You are not paying any attention to my needs at all! Thank You for reminding me of your patience.

Search me and know my heart, that I might not harbor anything in my life that keeps me from Your ordained perfect health. Also, I believe my life and healing will be a testimony to Your great love. May it lead others to come to believe in You and Your mighty saving grace, that they, too, may be saved and healed.

Thank You, Lord, for honoring me with this task. Thank You for Your patience toward me!

In Jesus' name, I pray. Amen.

40. ROMANS 8:11 NIV

AND IF THE SPIRIT OF HIM WHO RAISED JESUS FROM THE DEAD IS LIVING IN YOU, HE WHO RAISED CHRIST FROM THE DEAD WILL ALSO GIVE LIFE TO YOUR MORTAL BODIES BECAUSE OF HIS SPIRIT WHO LIVES IN YOU.

Selah

Oh, Holy Spirit of God, how mighty You are, raising Jesus from the dead. To think You are living in me to give me life in my mortal body. You raise me from being dead in the Law and alive in Christ. What joy!

I want to meditate on how You give me life in my body, just as it is. You never ask me to come to You perfect or already whole. You meet me where I am.

You love me enough to raise me from my illness, just as You raised Jesus and fulfilled prophecy for Him and also for me. May the name of the Lord be praised forever.

In Jesus' name, Amen.

---

41. PROVERBS 17:22 NLT

A CHEERFUL HEART IS A GOOD MEDICINE, BUT A BROKEN SPIRIT SAPS A PERSON'S STRENGTH.

SELAH

Lord, give me a truly cheerful heart. I have felt my own broken spirit dry up my bones. I have felt that brokenness down deep inside me. Only Your being gives me strength to go on. This is something to be cheerful about. I can use that good medicine! This is the gift of salvation. This is why You came and died for me, that I might live and give testimony.

My testimony is about Your goodness and eternal lovingkindness. King Solomon truly had great wisdom from You, Lord. May Your wisdom dwell in me regarding my life and health.

In Jesus' mighty and joyous name. Amen.

42. MATTHEW 10:8 NIV

Heal the sick, raise the dead, cleanse those who have leprosy, drive out demons. Freely you have received; freely give.

Selah

Dearest Father, You make Your will known to us plainly. Healing the sick and raising the dead, cleansing leprosy, and driving out demons are gifts of the Holy Spirit given to us to have power over the enemy in our bodies.

Jesus truly was sent to deliver... and sickness was a major factor. He healed thousands in His lifetime. He surely wants to deliver me from my illness, too. I praise You, Father God. I praise You, Jesus. I praise You, Holy Spirit. You walked the earth showing compassion to all You met.

I thank You for having this compassion toward me. I ask that You send prayer warriors my way that freely give, as they have been given to freely. Thank You for Your servants, Lord, who work through the Holy Spirit to bring life and health to me.

Dear Father, I thank You and pray in Jesus' mighty name. Amen.

43. JONAH 2:8–9 BSB

Those who regard vain idols forsake their faithfulness, But I will sacrifice to You with the voice of thanksgiving. That which I have vowed I will pay. Salvation is from the Lord.

Selah

"*That which I vowed I will pay.*" How many times have I neglected my promises to You? More than I can count. I can't keep my promises without Your Spirit. I have no wooden idols, but I do have my streaming movies and games, hobbies, and other activities of life's distractions.

Not that You begrudge me these pastimes, only that I have neglected my worship and prayer to You. I became numb in doing what I want, not what I have made promises to You to fulfill. Forgive me, Lord.

Thank You that when we confess our sins You throw them into the sea of forgetfulness and see us in the righteousness of Jesus instead. You give me a clean slate to start over out of Your love for me.

I do love You and instead of making vows, I'll just follow Jesus and love You with all my heart. You will lead me in His path of righteousness.

All glory to You!

In Jesus' name, Amen.

44. ISAIAH 19:22 NIV

SEE NOW THAT I AM HE; THERE IS NO GOD BESIDES ME. I BRING DEATH AND I GIVE LIFE; I WOUND AND I HEAL, AND THERE IS NO ONE WHO CAN DELIVER FROM MY HAND.

Selah

Father, I know that You were writing to the rebellious nations of Israel and Judah. I know that You are He and there is no God besides You. Still, in the midst of such grievous sins, You sent Jesus to fulfill Your law.

You were willing to forgo Your anger over the Israelites in forsaking their love for You for other gods who were no gods.

You sent Jesus to fulfill the Law, show Your love, heal and restore the lost of Your sheep. You made a way for the whole world to be saved. Jesus came to seek and save the lost.

Thank you, Jesus, for seeking and saving this needy one of Your sheep. I am forever grateful for your salvation and sacrifice.

In Your name, I pray, Jesus. Amen.

45. MATTHEW 6:34 AMP

So do not worry about tomorrow; for tomorrow will worry about itself. Each day has enough trouble of its own.

Selah

Dear Father, worrying is something that I often do, even when I am not really aware of it. I find myself talking in my head to myself, or others about the future concerns I have about life, the state of the country or the world, my family, and my personal condition. I'm stressing over that which I cannot control. I do all this instead of taking my deep concerns to You immediately. I let anxiety take hold and I forget about Your deliverance.

How could I forget? Well, of course, that enemy is prowling about, and then there is my weakness. I do remember that although my flesh is willing, my flesh is so weak. Lord, strengthen my spirit according to Your pleasure when I seek Your face. I want the Holy Spirit to bring to mind that I don't need to worry about tomorrow. Please set a guard over my lips, Holy Spirit that I may speak the words you author and not mine. I want to sing praise instead of spending too much time in my head with worry. I want to give You glory instead of worrying about this world and what *could* happen.

You are so right when You say that today has enough trouble of its own. Right now, I feel especially weak in mind and body. I feel like I could drown in sorrows, but I know you are with me. I hold onto that. As the Psalmist says, you make me lie down in green pastures, you lead me beside quiet waters and You restore my soul.

What more can I ask for than Your tender loving care? With this thought, I lie down in peace to sleep and receive Your blessings that You have ordained since days of old.

In Jesus' name I pray and give thanks. Amen.

46. REVELATION 21:4 KJV

AND GOD SHALL WIPE AWAY ALL TEARS FROM THEIR EYES; AND THERE SHALL BE NO MORE DEATH, NEITHER SORROW, NOR CRYING, NEITHER SHALL THERE BE ANY MORE PAIN: FOR THE FORMER THINGS ARE PASSED AWAY.

Selah

Lord, Your promise to comfort me, take away sorrow and pain, and even death is worth putting my hope in. My life has become a vale of tears, with death shadowing me. Sorrow and crying have often been my daily bread.

If I am to leave this earth, if it is my time to go, I look to You. But only then am I ready. I will not go by my own hand or that of another. I will not give up one moment of the time You have allotted to me.

You said there is an appointed time for a man to die. I don't want one second of the life You have for me stolen away by Satan. You lead me to a new place filled with freedom because these horrid things have passed away and I have reached my real life and home.

Thank You for Your promise and Your peace. I have all fear removed because You have made plain what my future will bring. All praise to You, my God!

In Jesus' name, Amen.

47. 1 KINGS 8:37–39 KJV

If there be in the land famine, if there be pestilence, if there be blasting or mildew, locust or caterpillar; if their enemy besiege them in the land of their cities; whatsoever plague, whatsoever sickness there be; whatever prayer, whatever supplication is made by anyone, or by all Your people Israel, when each one knows the plague of his own heart and spreads out his hands toward this temple; Then hear thou in heaven thy dwelling place, and forgive, and do, and give to every man according to his ways, whose heart thou knowest; (for thou, even thou only, knowest the hearts of all the children of men;

Selah

Lord, You brought pestilence and famine to the land of Your promise in days of old as punishments for disloyalty. Oh, what a change Jesus bought for me in His new covenant. In the old covenant, the king implores You to hear the earnest prayers of Your people. He begs that You judge them one by one and not as the entire nation deserves.

Today You still reward me, one whose heart is turned toward You. You do not judge me according to our nation's actions. You do not judge me at all since in Jesus I am the very righteousness of God. Oh, thank You, Lord. Thank You.

King Solomon trusts in You. He knows You know all that people think and do. You know what I think and do. I cannot know how to live except by Your grace, and I fall on the grace and mercy You gave me in my Lord, Jesus Christ. I praise You, dear God!

I pray In Jesus' name, Amen.

48. ISAIAH 53:4 NASB

However, it was our sicknesses that He Himself bore, and our pains that He carried; yet we ourselves assumed that He had been afflicted, struck down by God, and humiliated.

Selah

He who bore my sicknesses Himself. This could not be plainer, Lord. Your pains You carried for me. Even though I know You, in my heart I have a hard time really understanding that *You* were afflicted, struck down by God, and humiliated in *my* place.

I have not fully comprehended that it was for the joy set before You that You endured this torture for me. I have not come to grips with the fact that it was for Freedom the Christ set us free. More than any mere man could endure, You bore Your terrible suffering silently.

You stood in my place, like the true Lamb of God You are. I can never repay You. All I can do is believe that You did all this for me and that the work is finished in Your death and resurrection. All glory to the God who saves! In Jesus' name, Amen.

49. LUKE 4:40–41 NLT

As the sun went down that evening, people throughout the village brought sick family members to Jesus. No matter what their diseases were, the touch of his hand healed every one. Many were possessed by demons; and the demons came out at his command, shouting, "You are the Son of God!" But because they knew he was the Messiah, he rebuked them and refused to let them speak.

Selah

Lord, From dawn to dusk You ministered to the sick. No matter what disease was presented, it was healed. The demons may have been the result of worshiping other gods since they were of demonic origin. Idols were not a part of God's plan for His people. I don't know why demons were so common, but it does not matter since this is Your secret. You never said why.

You had all authority over them. You demanded that they leave the possessed and even command that they be silent so that no one would hear that You are the Son of God. Now You have died in the flesh. Now You have risen in the flesh. You showed the whole world that You are the Son of God and Allowed the Father to send You dwell among us. I believe since Your Holy Spirit lives in me there is no room for demons.

I put on the full armor of God...the belt of truth, the breastplate of righteousness and love, the shoes of the preparation of the gospel of peace, and the helmet of salvation. Also, I take up the shield of faith and the sword of the Spirit that I may stand against the enemy who comes against me to wound and work evil against me.

Protect me in every way, Lord, against my enemies. I thank You and praise You for Your protection.

In Jesus' name, Amen.

CHAPTER SIX

The Word and the Guided Prayer

Part 3

50. 2 CHRONICLES 16:9 NASB

For the eyes of the LORD move to and fro throughout the earth that He may strongly support those whose heart is completely His.

Selah

How I praise You for strongly supporting me. My heart is, by the power of the Holy Spirit, completely Yours. I praise You that as Your eyes move to and fro, no matter where I go, You are watching over me to make sure I am protected.

You hold me up in my weaknesses. You draw me ever closer to You, Lord, so that Your word becomes living and active in me. Please keep strongly supporting me so that my heart is guarded.

Thank You for keeping me completely Yours. Thank You, Thank You, Thank You!

In Jesus' name, Amen.

51. MATTHEW 9:20–22 BSB

And a woman who had been suffering from a hemorrhage for twelve years came up behind Him and touched the fringe of His cloak; for she was saying to herself, "If I only touch His garment, I will get well." But Jesus turning and seeing her said, "Daughter, take courage; your faith has made you well." At once the woman was made well.

Selah

Take courage! Take courage! My faith has and is making me well. When I touch the hem of Jesus' garment, I am made whole and healed. In God, there is no separation of time and space.

His grace and healing virtue is the same yesterday, today, and tomorrow. I can still touch the hem of his garment in the Spirit. I notice that this woman suffered 12 long and painful years, being unclean according to the Law.

I thank You that no matter what degree or type of illness I have, You never call me unclean because I am cleansed through the broken, sacrificed body and blood of Jesus.

Thank You, Jesus, for coming to fulfill the Law so that I can be free. Something to definitely inspire courage! All glory to Your holy name.

In Jesus' name, I pray, Amen.

52. PSALM 3:1B–3 BSB

I WILL EXALT YOU, O LORD, FOR YOU HAVE LIFTED ME UP AND HAVE NOT ALLOWED MY FOES TO REJOICE OVER ME. LORD MY GOD, I CRIED TO YOU FOR HELP, AND YOU HEALED ME. LORD, YOU PULLED ME UP FROM SHEOL; YOU SPARED ME FROM DESCENDING INTO THE PIT...

Selah

Oh, Father, I do exalt You. I praise Your majestic name and give You the praise and glory You deserve. You lift me up. You do not allow my enemy to rejoice over destroying me in the work of Jesus. I cry to you for help and you heal me.

You never leave me to the hands of destruction and You save me from going down to that horrible pit of darkness without You. Still, it's so hard to get out of the place of darkness. Jesus, You are the light, so with You leading me, I will not walk in darkness ever again.

Your mercy spares me. Your grace saves me. Your death and resurrection have bought my life. No matter which side of this earth I am, because of You, Jesus, I will never see death. I will never go down to the pit.

I praise and thank You, Father. In Jesus' name, I pray. Amen

53. JEREMIAH 17:14 NLT

Lord, if You heal me, I will be truly healed; if You save me, I will be truly saved. My praises are for You alone!

Selah

This verse, Lord God, says it all.

When You heal me, then no illness, disease, or condition can un-heal me or un-save me. I am truly saved. I am truly healed.

How much You have demonstrated Your love in the Word, from the first to the last. I give praise to God the Father, Jesus the Son, and the Holy Spirit.

My praises are to You forever. I pray in Jesus' name. Amen.

54. JOEL 3:10 KJV

Beat your plowshares into swords, and your pruning hooks into spears: let the weak say, I am strong.

Selah

Lord, Your directives for weapons of warfare to those who feel they have none are definite. Use the sharpest tools I have already and make them weapons fit to defeat the enemy. Use my "farm tools" of weakness to prove Your strength.

I have no reason to feel undefended when I am at my weakest. The weapons of warfare I use are spiritual, sharper than any 2-edged sword. My armor protects me in this battle. Thank You for making sure I am equipped for the task and fight at hand.

When I am weak, I will say I am strong. I will be strong because I use the weapons of the Word of God to fight with. I will be courageous because You are always with me and You train my hands for war. Thank You for always taking care of me.

I pray in Jesus' name. Amen.

55. MARK 5:40-42A BSB

AND THEY LAUGHED AT HIM. AFTER HE HAD PUT THEM ALL OUTSIDE, HE TOOK THE CHILD'S FATHER AND MOTHER AND HIS OWN COMPANIONS AND WENT IN TO SEE THE CHILD. TAKING HER BY THE HAND, JESUS SAID, "TALITHA KOUM!" WHICH MEANS "LITTLE GIRL, I SAY TO YOU, GET UP!" IMMEDIATELY THE GIRL GOT UP AND BEGAN TO WALK AROUND.

Selah

How compassionate You are, Jesus. How loving that You turned aside from where You were going, pushing Your way through crowds and going to see a little girl who just died. She wasn't dead to You, was she? She was just waiting to see You.

I take Your hand so that I, too, may receive that healing virtue that You have from the Father. This lives on today through Your sacrifice on the cross where You bore my sickness, disease, and sorrows, through the Holy Spirit.

I pray in Your name, Jesus. Amen.

____

____

____

____

____

____

56. MALACHI 4:2 AMP

BUT FOR YOU WHO FEAR MY NAME [WITH AWE-FILLED REVERENCE] THE SUN OF RIGHTEOUSNESS WILL RISE WITH HEALING IN ITS WINGS. AND YOU WILL GO FORWARD AND LEAP [JOYFULLY] LIKE CALVES [RELEASED] FROM THE STALL.

Selah

I fear Your name, my Lord. Holy and awe-struck fear, not the cowardly kind.

Who else created and controls the earth with all its splendors and terrors? Only You. Your majesty rules and reigns through all creation. There is no one like You in heaven or on earth.

You say the sun of righteousness will rise with healing in its wings. This seems like You are saying that as the sun rises each new day that there is again healing in the sun's rays (wings). You also seem to say the Son sends healing and righteousness in each new day. How wonderful that Your healing comes anew day by day. Day by day You remember that I am in need and You are taking care of me...every day.

As I progress in my healing, I will remember that You send healing each day. I wait and hope for the faith to carry out the times and tasks that You have set before me now. Thank You, Lord. I pray in Jesus' name. Amen.

57. JEREMIAH 33:6 KJV

NEVERTHELESS, I WILL BRING TO IT (JERUSALEM) HEALTH AND HEALING, AND I WILL HEAL ITS PEOPLE AND REVEAL TO THEM THE ABUNDANCE OF PEACE AND TRUTH. I WILL RESTORE JUDAH AND ISRAEL FROM CAPTIVITY AND WILL REBUILD THEM AS IN FORMER TIMES. AND I WILL CLEANSE THEM FROM ALL THE INIQUITY THEY HAVE COMMITTED AGAINST ME, AND WILL FORGIVE ALL THEIR SINS.

Selah

Oh Father, how You hated that You had to punish Your people of old for following idols. They were breaking the Law and great were their sins toward You. Your mercy toward them afterward was undeserved, for sure. Still today, Your mercy triumphs over justice.

What a beautiful foreshadowing picture of Jesus' life. He brought healing, peace, and truth to me by the Holy Spirit. You established the Kingdom of God here on earth lost through Adam's sin!

Thank You, Lord, for sending Jesus to do away with the punishment I also deserve. Because of the sacrifice of Jesus, the Lamb of God, I, too, am shown Your mercy and grace even when I have sinned. I am not seen by You as a sinner, but the righteousness of God in my Savior, Christ.

I stand by Your right side in Jesus, and Your purity and love move You to favor me with things, like healing, that I do not deserve. I am so grateful to receive from Your hand, Lord God.

In Jesus' name, I pray. Amen.

58. LUKE 15:4 NLT

IF A MAN HAS A HUNDRED SHEEP AND ONE OF THEM GETS LOST, WHAT WILL HE DO? WON'T HE LEAVE THE NINETY-NINE OTHERS IN THE WILDERNESS AND GO TO SEARCH FOR THE ONE THAT IS LOST UNTIL HE FINDS IT?

Selah

Lord, thank You for when I get lost, You search me out and return me to the fold. You never leave me or forsake me. You are willing to leave the others of Your flock to rescue me because they will be safe in Your love and tender care in their green pastures.

It does not matter that You leave the ninety-nine. You know that they will be safe together. All I know is that I am worth as much as they are to You. You value me that much.

When I am doubting, or turning my back on You because I have not gotten the healing I asked for yet, You still seek me. You get me out of trouble. Thank You for not giving up until You find me and return me to the safety of Your flock.

Thank You for bringing me into Your healthy pastures. Thank You for watching over me so I don't go astray anymore. I am humbled and grateful. I give You thanks for Your great mercy. I pray in Your name, Jesus. Amen.

59. PSALMS 42:11 KJV

WHY ART THOU CAST DOWN, O MY SOUL? AND WHY ART THOU DISQUIETED WITHIN ME? HOPE THOU IN GOD: FOR I SHALL YET PRAISE HIM, WHO IS THE HEALTH OF MY COUNTENANCE, AND MY GOD.

Selah

Yes, today I am downcast in secret ways. I can put on a happy face, but I can't really remember the last time I was truly cheerful. I can't recall the last time the joy of the Lord filled me.

I know this isn't going to cut it if I am waiting for my healing. Jesus. Having unbelief hinders Your work in me. I need Your Holy Spirit to guide me.

If I was able to dredge up this hope and joy by myself, I would. I need You to lead me here. I will listen to Your words to praise You. King David says, by Your Holy Spirit that You are the health of my countenance.

Dear Father God, I again say, I hope in You. I meditate on the many ways You have made me glad before. I count my many blessings. I believe that I am Your righteousness, Your right and straight standing in this world, in Jesus.

And in Jesus's name, I pray. Amen.

60. PROVERBS 4:20-23 NASB

MY SON, GIVE ATTENTION TO MY WORDS; INCLINE YOUR EAR TO MY SAYINGS. DO NOT LET THEM DEPART FROM YOUR SIGHT; KEEP THEM IN THE MIDST OF YOUR HEART. FOR THEY ARE LIFE TO THOSE WHO FIND THEM AND HEALTH TO ALL THEIR BODY. WATCH OVER YOUR HEART WITH ALL DILIGENCE, FOR FROM IT FLOW THE SPRINGS OF LIFE.

Selah

Again, Lord, I am hearing about words. So, I incline my ears to Your sayings and I will not let them out of my sight. I will keep the Word in my heart.

Yes, I believe they are life to those who find them and health to all my body. Yes, I will watch over my heart to let no evil thought take root there. From my heart, my inner being, flow Your springs of life, as You told the woman at the well.

Thank You, Jesus. I pray in Your name. Amen.

61. LUKE 7:2-10 NIV

So, Jesus went with them. He was not far from the house when the centurion sent friends to say to him: "Lord, don't trouble yourself, for I do not deserve to have you come under my roof. That is why I did not even consider myself worthy to come to you. But say the word, and my servant will be healed. For I myself am a man under authority, with soldiers under me. I tell this one, 'Go,' and he goes; and that one, 'Come,' and he comes. I say to my servant, 'Do this,' and he does it." When Jesus heard this, he was amazed at him, and turning to the crowd following him, he said, "I tell you, I have not found such great faith even in Israel." Then the men who had been sent returned to the house and found the servant well.

Selah

Such great faith was not found among the people of God. Here, Jesus again has compassion for a Gentile. The centurion believed so much, he said not to bother Himself going to his house.

Lord, I know faith is in short supply today. Certainly, my faith can use a boost. Thank You for Your word to give me that extra lift up. I have found that even though I have heard to believe in you, that is still a difficult prospect without Your Holy Spirit to strengthen me.

Facing my health challenge is hard when I hear diagnoses. Friends and even pastors say things that are contrary to Your word. I do not reject the treatment I must have but I don't have to accept the projected outcomes from anyone except You and Your word.

I praise You for making the way for the impossible of man to be Your possibility. All things are possible with You. Thank You and I pray in Your name, Jesus. Amen.

62. ISAIAH 35:3-7 NIV

Say to those with fearful hearts, "Be strong, do not fear; Your God will come, he will come with vengeance; with divine retribution, he will come to save you." Then will the eyes of the blind be opened and the ears of the deaf unstopped. Then will the lame leap like a deer, and the mute tongue shout for joy.

Selah

Lord, I am amazed at how much revelation You gave to Isaiah to write down about the coming of our Savior. Everything he says here happened when Jesus walked the earth.

So, by Your Power, the Holy Spirit strengthens my weak hands and feeble knees. I say to my anxious heart, "Be strong and do not fear. Behold my God will come with vengeance to the evil enemies that pursue me to make me doubt You."

To this day these things still apply because You are the same yesterday, today, and tomorrow. I shout with joy! I may whisper my shout, but I shout all the same. You are worthy of all praise.

I pray in Your name, dearest Jesus. Amen.

63. JEREMIAH 30:16 KJV

Therefore, all they that devour thee shall be devoured; and all thine adversaries, every one of them, shall go into captivity; and they that spoil thee shall be a spoil, and all that prey upon thee will I give for a prey.

Selah

I know You are talking about evil powers and principalities that have come against me. But, here in Your word, it says that every single one of them will be devoured, made a spoil of war, and that they will go into captivity. All those who come to devour me will be devoured.

I am aware and I put on the full armor of God that I may stand as You send Your angel armies to fight for me. I take shelter under Your wings. Hallelujah!

I praise and thank You, Jesus, in Your name I pray. Amen.

64. EZEKIEL 34:16A NASB

I WILL SEEK THE LOST, BRING BACK THE SCATTERED, BIND UP THE BROKEN, AND STRENGTHEN THE SICK.

Selah

Thank You for seeking me in my lost state. Thank You for bringing me back from those with whom I have been scattered. I know that even churches can become scattered for different reasons, but thank You for seeking and saving us all.

Thank You for binding up my brokenness and strengthening me in my sickness. Thank You for pouring in the oil and the wine as the Good Samaritan did, my Great Physician.

I glorify Your Holy Name in the highest. Praises and thanks in Your name, Jesus. Amen.

65. MATTHEW 14:35–36 NASB

AND WHEN THE MEN OF THAT PLACE RECOGNIZED HIM, THEY SENT WORD INTO ALL THAT SURROUNDING REGION AND BROUGHT TO HIM ALL WHO WERE SICK; AND THEY PLEADED WITH HIM THAT THEY MIGHT JUST TOUCH THE BORDER OF HIS CLOAK; AND ALL WHO TOUCHED IT WERE CURED.

Selah

Lord, the word went out. Your miracles caused men to run to You. You spoke the words of life over the sick. Even Your garments were imbued with Your power.

I have to believe that Your healing virtue exists for me today. I close my eyes now and see You looking at me and saying, "Just reach out in faith and touch me." Your healing for me is assured.

You live in me and I live in You. Your life is in me and my life is in You. I can rest in Your presence as I praise You.

Thank You! In Your name, I pray, Jesus. Amen.

66. PROVERBS 15:4 KJV

A wholesome tongue is a tree of life: but perverseness therein is a breach in the spirit.

Selah

Such a short verse that says so much.

Lord, give me that wholesome tongue that speaks Your Word by the Power of the Holy Spirit. Your truth and Your love give me life and I receive it with my whole being.

Let perversion and bitterness and anger and revenge be far from me. I want my tongue to be a tree of life.

A breach in my spirit, a torn brokenness is not something that will easily heal without Your intervention, Lord. I want wholeness, I will keep Your word, by Your power, through the Holy Spirit, Jesus.

And in Your name, I pray. Amen.

67. ISAIAH 53:4–5 BSB

Surely, He took on our infirmities and carried our sorrows; yet we considered Him stricken by God, struck down and afflicted. But He was pierced for our transgressions, He was crushed for our iniquities; the punishment that brought us peace was upon Him, and by His stripes, we are healed.

Selah

How graphic a depiction of Your purpose on the cross, Jesus. How You did this, I just don't know. The Father's love propelled You there, but even for a short while, he forsook You.

Still, for the joy set before You, You endured the cross. Your joy at seeing us set free from our sicknesses, our pains, our wrongdoings, and the punishment of our well-being was laid on You. By Your wounds, Lord Jesus, we are healed.

But the Father caused all my wrongdoing to fall on Jesus. So now, in You, Jesus, I am the righteousness of God. Cleansed and forgiven by the love and grace of God.

Thank You, Jesus. I'm so grateful for Your ultimate sacrifice and I can't wait until I see You face-to-face so I can praise You forever.

In Your name of Power, Might, and Glory, Jesus. Amen.

68. MARK 3:9A NLT

JESUS INSTRUCTED HIS DISCIPLES TO HAVE A BOAT READY SO THE CROWD WOULD NOT CRUSH HIM. HE HAD HEALED MANY PEOPLE THAT DAY, SO ALL THE SICK PEOPLE EAGERLY PUSHED FORWARD TO TOUCH HIM.

Selah

Jesus, You are the Son of Man as well as the Son of God. Father, those who wanted miracles were about to crush Your Son. By the Holy Spirit, He was prepared for the unbelieving masses. The sick, the possessed, they all wanted a touch.

Still, didn't You say to them to only believe, and they will be healed? The crowd was left behind. It looks like they didn't really take the believing part to heart.

He rebuked people because they needed a sign to believe. I, too, have to believe Your word, Lord. I don't want to be left on the shore with no recourse because I didn't trust You.

There is no other Name in heaven and earth by which I can be saved. So, I will not stand on the shore pushing toward You in unbelief and missing Your blessing. I will rest in Your grace and power and believe in my healing. Praise to Your Holy Name, Jesus.

By faith, I pray and I win in Your precious name, Jesus. Amen.

69. NUMBERS 23:19 NLT

God is not a man, so he does not lie. He is not human, so he does not change his mind. Has he ever spoken and failed to act? Has he ever promised and not carried it through?

Selah

Dear God, how I thank You that You do not lie. It is not possible in Your holiness to have any deceit. I hear You now that when You speak, You do not fail to act.

Jesus, who is Son of man and He who dwells as one in You, can have no deceit. When You have spoken forth Your word on healing, You *cannot* lie. You will not ever fail to act.

You have promised and You will carry it through according to Your word, which never fails. Thank You, Lord, for such reassurance, love, and true grace. Thank You that as it is done in heaven, so it will be done on earth when You have spoken.

All Glory to You, Lord.

I pray in Jesus' name for myself, my family, and those who need it most right now. Amen.

70. DEUTERONOMY 7:14–15A KJV

THOU SHALT BE BLESSED ABOVE ALL PEOPLE: THERE SHALL NOT BE MALE OR FEMALE BARREN AMONG YOU, OR AMONG YOUR CATTLE. THE LORD WILL KEEP YOU FREE FROM EVERY DISEASE. HE WILL NOT INFLICT ON YOU THE HORRIBLE DISEASES YOU KNEW IN EGYPT.

Selah

Oh, Father, again You speak Your blessings over me. To say I will be blessed above all people is astounding. The Israelites of old didn't deserve these words of blessing any more than I do today, even though they were Your holy people. They were supposed to keep the Law to obtain these blessings, but they did not.

Today I do not have to live by the strict, stringent Law. I do not because Jesus fulfilled the Law that would keep me bound and enslaved.

Only in Jesus is the grace You planned from the day Moses wrote these words. Only in Jesus are You able to keep me free from every disease because He stood in my place on the cross to pay for my wrongdoing.

Only His sacrifice makes any sense in Your lovingkindness towards me. Only in the grace, You extend because of Jesus' sacrifice are You willing to protect me from the horrible diseases I knew before I entered into Your Kingdom. Thank You for salvation, Lord.

Thank you! In Jesus' name, I pray. Amen.

71. MATTHEW 15:22-29 BSB

And a Canaanite woman from that region came to Him, crying out, "Lord, Son of David, have mercy on me! My daughter is miserably possessed by a demon." But Jesus did not answer a word. So His disciples came and urged Him, "Send her away, for she keeps crying out after us." He answered, "I was sent only to the lost sheep of the house of Israel. The woman came and knelt before Him. "Lord, help me!" she said. But Jesus replied, "It is not right to take the children's bread and toss it to the dogs." "Yes, Lord," she said, " even the dogs eat the crumbs that fall from their master's table." "O woman," Jesus answered, "your faith is great! Let it be done for you as you desire." And her daughter was healed from that very hour.

Selah

Sometimes I feel like the dog under the table. Sometimes I don't even feel worthy of the children's bread. Sometimes I feel less than a lost sheep. You don't feel that way though, Lord. You came to die for me so that I would have value in this world. I would be clean and be, in Jesus, Your righteousness.

Even with an unbeliever, an unclean person, You rewarded the faith of this Canaanite woman. How much more do You want me to believe, since You have called me not only a lost sheep but Your child, worthy of Your bread at the table because I am a child of God by grace. Lord. I cry out "Help my unbelief."

In Your name, Jesus, I pray. Amen.

72. 2 KINGS 4:27-34 BSB

When Elisha reached the house, there was the boy lying dead on his bed. So, he went in, closed the door behind the two of them, and prayed to the LORD. Then Elisha got on the bed and lay on the boy, mouth to mouth, eye to eye, and hand to hand. As he stretched himself out over him, the boy's body became warm. Elisha turned away and paced back and forth across the room. Then he got on the bed and stretched himself out over the boy again, and the boy sneezed seven times and opened his eyes.

Selah

What a beautiful picture You paint here, Lord. The man of God prayed to You. Then he got on the bed and fit himself to the dead boy. When the boy grew warm, Elisha walked around, no doubt praying in the Spirit.

Then he did it again. But he didn't just depend on his first prayer to You. He took action as directed by Your Spirit. He did not just try lying once on the young man, and then give up. He did it again after more time to seek Your face and will and directives.

Lord, give me the patience to receive Your healing just the way You want it. I know Your life-giving power does not come because of my own merits but through Your love for me. Thank You, Lord, for making a way for me to find healing, even though it might come in stages. Or through the intervention of someone (or many) to give aid.

Help me, by Your Holy Spirit, to remember that Your ways are not my ways and that in the right time Your healing love will reveal itself. I surrender myself to Your will.

I pray in the name of Jesus. Amen.

73. 2 CHRONICLES 6:14 NLT

HE (KING SOLOMON) PRAYED, "O LORD, GOD OF ISRAEL, THERE IS NO GOD LIKE YOU IN ALL OF HEAVEN AND EARTH. YOU KEEP YOUR COVENANT AND SHOW UNFAILING LOVE TO ALL WHO WALK BEFORE YOU IN WHOLEHEARTED DEVOTION.

Selah

Oh, my Father, *"there is no god like You in heaven and earth."* How this sings to my soul! There is no place I need to turn other than You. There is no hope to place in that which is not ordained by You.

There are no words from those who do not know Your will that I have to take in. I have on the helmet of salvation. It keeps me from false words and even well-intentioned things that are spoken to me that are not authored by the Holy Spirit.

I know this is through the grace of Jesus Christ. Without the power of His Holy Spirit, I have failed again and again to walk before You in wholehearted devotion. Thank You for sending Jesus to die so that I might live. Thank You for listening to my prayers, no matter what, because I am Your child.

All honor to You in the precious name of Jesus Christ. Amen.

---

74. PROVERBS 3:1-2 KJV

My son, forget not my law; but let thine heart keep my commandments: For length of days, and long life, and peace, shall they add to thee.

Selah

Thank You, Father, for King Solomon's words to his son. As a King, he had the right to issue commands to his son. How much more do You have the right to issue the commands in the Law.

But Jesus has overcome the law of sin and death. This shows that when my heart rejoices in You, You rejoice in me and give me blessings I cannot earn. Length of days, and long life. What a promise! Your peace You will add to me.

I can use an extra measure of peace when I face trials of sickness and disease. I am grateful that Jesus bore all my sorrows and pain. He bought my health with his stripes. I believe because Your word says over and over that You love me and take care of me.

Thank You in Jesus' mighty name. Amen.

CHAPTER SEVEN

The Word and the Guided Prayer

Part 4

75. MATTHEW 11:29 NASB

TAKE MY YOKE UPON YOU AND LEARN FROM ME, FOR I AM GENTLE AND HUMBLE IN HEART, AND YOU WILL FIND REST FOR YOUR SOULS.

Selah

"Gentle and humble." What a promise to find rest for my soul without fear of punishment or of being too great a burden to You. Your yoke is easy, and Your burden is light. Whether I face sickness, addiction, disease, depression, or other physical or mental problems, this is but a lesson. You want to teach me to be an overcomer.

You tell me that when I am weary and tired of the world, You have an answer that restores me. Sometimes I am tired of living in this pain and want to give up. How wonderful to know that by embracing the momentary situation (for You do want it to be temporary) that I will find the rest and comfort that my soul needs. I will be relieved and like You, gentle and humble in heart. From my inner being, I will find contentment in Your presence, because You carried my true sufferings on Your cross.

I am so thankful, Lord and in Your name, I pray. Amen.

76. ISAIAH 58:8 KJV

THEN SHALL THY LIGHT BREAK FORTH AS THE MORNING, AND THINE HEALTH SHALL SPRING FORTH SPEEDILY: AND THY RIGHTEOUSNESS SHALL GO BEFORE THEE; THE GLORY OF THE LORD SHALL BE THY REWARD.

Selah

Oh, Lord, how I love that through the sacrifice of Jesus my light will break through like the morning, and my healing will spring forth speedily. What a wonderful picture of the rewards of believing in Jesus. How gracious You are to speak of this in the time of Isaiah, hundreds of years before His work was accomplished.

This is a true measure of Your love for me, and a promise that has stood the test of time. How wonderful to have my light in You break forth like the dawn, as the new day sun rises. I do want to shine like this, regardless of my situation.

I want the people around me–my family, my health providers, my friends, and even strangers I may meet–to notice this bright light of God change in me. I want to share Your love and goodness toward me. Thank You, Father.

I pray in the name of Jesus. Amen.

77. 1 PETER 2:24 NLT

He personally carried our sins in his body on the cross so that we can be dead to sin and live for what is right. By his wounds, you are healed.

Selah

Jesus, You are the One who personally carried my sins in Your own body on the Cross. This was the greatest sacrifice ever known in the world. I can never fully understand what this was like. I can never know how You felt, taking not only my sin but the sins of the whole world on Yourself.

You knew, though, what it was going to cost. You knew You would be despised and rejected. You knew those You loved most would be scattered each to their own house. You knew You would be all alone in Your suffering.

How I feel like this is very like my own situation now, even though I know it is not even remotely the same. Still, I feel alone when I don't keep my mind on You. I feel pity for myself often, when the pain is so great until I remember how much You suffered that I might live.

No one can really know how it is I'm feeling. No one can know how to heal me. No one can carry this burden for me. No one, that is, except for You.

In You, I can be dead to sin. In You, I can live for what is right. In You, my body is healed because Your wounds made it so.

In Your name, I pray, Jesus. Amen.

78. PSALMS 80:18–19 BSB

Then we will not turn away from You; revive us, and we will call on Your name. Restore us, O Lord God of Hosts; Cause Your face to shine upon us, that we may be saved.

Selah

Father God, You have given me Jesus, so I will not turn away from You. You give me no reason to be ashamed. I come as I am because I am Your righteousness in Jesus. There is nothing You see but Your own Glory that Jesus won at the cross.

I call on Your name, Daddy. Restore me to health and wholeness because You are the God of the angel armies. You can do exceedingly more than I ask or think.

It is Your face that shines on me when I look at You. This is how I come to shine in this world and give testimony of the love and grace and mercy of the Highest God.

I pray in the name of Jesus. Amen.

79. 1 PETER 5:5B–7 NLT

And all of you, dress yourselves in humility as you relate to one another, for "God opposes the proud but gives grace to the humble." So, humble yourselves under the mighty power of God, and at the right time he will lift you up in honor. Give all your worries and cares to God, for he cares about you.

Selah

Lord, if I could dress myself in Your humility, I would. It is only by Your Holy Spirit that I can do all things. The kind of humility You have, where You put aside Your heavenly majesty to come to this dirty, violent, and lost earth.

What love You show me! By Your Spirit, I do humble myself before You. I need Your grace to get through this time.

I look forward to the time where You lift me up in honor, showing the world Your mighty power to heal and to save.

I give You my worries. They do me no good, and You care for me, so I don't need to go there anyway.

All glorious praise to You, Lord. I pray in Jesus' name. Amen.

80. PSALM 88:1-2 NASB

LORD, THE GOD OF MY SALVATION, I HAVE CRIED OUT BY DAY AND IN THE NIGHT BEFORE YOU. LET MY PRAYER COME BEFORE YOU; INCLINE YOUR EAR TO MY CRY!

Selah

Oh, Abba Father, I do cry out to You day and night. I have faith that You hear me when I reach out to You. You are faithful and just, always loving me.

I do ask that my prayer come before You in the precious name of Jesus because He said He is the way to You. I cannot come before Your throne unless I come through Jesus.

I need Your healing and comfort for my body, mind, and spirit. I wait for You to answer my prayers. I wait patiently, knowing that all things work together for good to me because I love You. I am called according to Your purposes.

I believe one purpose for my life is to give testimony to the marvelous healing You are working in me.

I thank You, in the name of Jesus. Amen.

81. ISAIAH 33:2 KJV

LORD, BE GRACIOUS UNTO US; WE HAVE WAITED FOR THEE: BE THOU THEIR (MY) ARM EVERY MORNING, OUR (MY) SALVATION ALSO IN THE TIME OF TROUBLE.

SELAH

How gracious You are to me, Lord. I have and do wait for You. Waiting in peace and quiet comforts my soul. Anxiety, be gone! You have no part in me. Jesus, the Prince of Peace has brought grace and mercy to me.

Your arm is mighty, Lord, where mine is so weak, but You hold me with it every morning, every afternoon, and every night. You do exceedingly more than we can ask or think.

Thank You for being my salvation in this time of trouble. I know You do not despise my weaknesses, as some do. Rather, You say in Your word that strength is perfected in weakness.

So, with Paul, I glory in suffering, hardship, and weakness so that You may be glorified in all my ways.

In Jesus' name, I pray. Amen.

82. MATTHEW 19:26 NLT

JESUS LOOKED AT THEM INTENTLY AND SAID, "HUMANLY SPEAKING, IT IS IMPOSSIBLE. BUT WITH GOD EVERYTHING IS POSSIBLE."

Selah

You looked at them intently, Jesus. This was and is so important to understand. Sometimes I think I am in charge. But I am sorely mistaken.

I seek healing, and I have to lean on Your every word. When other healing methods don't work, I have a tendency to want to give up. Holy Spirit, work in me. Help me to truly give up the reins of my life.

Jesus is plain. Humanly speaking, so much of life is impossible. I cannot heal myself, and no one else can, either. Only with God is everything possible. Thank You, Jesus, for bringing this message to me. I am so grateful.

I pray in Your name, Jesus. Amen.

83. MARK 6:12–13 NASB

So the disciples went out, telling everyone they met to repent of their sins and turn to God. And they cast out many demons and healed many sick people, anointing them with olive oil.

Selah

Repentance. What a beautiful word, Lord! You gave me the right and privilege of turning away from sin by the Word of God and the gift of the Holy Spirit after the Cross redeemed us. The people the apostles met on the way didn't know you, Jesus. They didn't know You were the Messiah. They didn't know what Your mission was, nor how much You loved them.

For miracles to follow when the disciples preached repentance is another step above what the Baptist was showing people. Indeed, how You lift me up to another level with Your transformative Word.

How kind You were and are to send out messengers to tell Your story. I thank You for all those You send in my life telling of Your surpassing greatness.

Thank You, Lord. I am waiting expectantly for the anointing oil from the throne room. You bought this for me with Your death and resurrection.

I pray in the mighty name of Jesus. Amen.

84. ACTS 9:17–19 NIV

THEN ANANIAS WENT TO THE HOUSE AND ENTERED IT. PLACING HIS HANDS ON SAUL, HE SAID, "BROTHER SAUL, THE LORD—JESUS, WHO APPEARED TO YOU ON THE ROAD AS YOU WERE COMING HERE—HAS SENT ME SO THAT YOU MAY SEE AGAIN AND BE FILLED WITH THE HOLY SPIRIT." IMMEDIATELY, SOMETHING LIKE SCALES FELL FROM SAUL'S EYES, AND HE COULD SEE AGAIN. HE GOT UP AND WAS BAPTIZED,

Selah

Paul was blinded by Your glory, Lord. You obviously had a reason to let him wait three days to receive his sight back. He spent that time fasting and praying. I ask for the grace and mercy to fast and pray at Your direction, not in my own strength, but in Yours.

Ananias didn't want to lay hands on this former persecutor of the church. Still, he obeyed You. Let me obey You when I am reluctant to do Your will as shown to me by Your Word and the Holy Spirit.

Let me remember that baptism is a symbolic immersion into Your death and resurrection, a holy sacrament.

I thank You for all You do for me, Jesus, and in Your name, I pray. Amen.

85. LUKE 9:11 NLT

But the crowds found out where he was going, and they followed him. He welcomed them and taught them about the Kingdom of God, and he healed those who were sick.

Selah

I am one in the crowd, Lord. I am following after You to see the miracle of life that they all knew You had. I know You will speak the word of life to me in my heart. I believe You will an are healing me.

You welcome me. You whisper to me day and night through Your Holy Spirit about the Kingdom of God.

What joy it is to know that You have prepared a place for me in Your Kingdom!

Just as You did then, You do now. You heal me for I need healing. I put my trust and faith in You to see this work to completion.

In gratitude, I pray in Your name, Jesus. Amen.

86. JOHN 21:25 KJV

And there are also many other things which Jesus did, the which, if they should be written every one, I suppose that even the world itself could not contain the books that should be written. Amen.

Selah

Many other things. Many other things. As if the accounts of You are not enough, the apostle whom You loved, loves me by saying there are not enough books to hold all Your works and miracles.

I know You are the same yesterday, today, and tomorrow. There are more things You are doing that I just don't know about. I believe You are healing my mind, body, and spirit, even though I don't even have awareness of it.

There will be a day when You will reveal all. I wait for that day with anticipation and expectation. I look for healing in this world, for my mind and body, and spirit.

Thank You for all the works of God that You did to convince us, and for those, we have yet to know about.

I pray in Your name, Jesus. Amen.

87. EXODUS 15:2 KJV

THE LORD *IS* MY STRENGTH AND SONG, AND HE HAS BECOME MY SALVATION; HE *IS* MY GOD, AND I WILL PRAISE HIM; MY FATHER'S GOD, AND I WILL EXALT HIM.

Selah

I remember the old gospel song that sings of this scripture. I remember how good it feels for You to be my Strength and Song. I remember now that I can sing it again to be once again in Your presence, exalting You. I can be in Your presence, Father because Jesus made the way.

How You love me! You Left Your Word so that I, through the power of the Holy Spirit, would remember. I ask for even more of You in my life. I know this is my task because You are here without measure. Help me believe more, Holy Spirit.

I pray in Jesus' name. Amen.

88. PSALMS 119:107 NASB

I HAVE SUFFERED MUCH; PRESERVE MY LIFE, LORD, ACCORDING TO YOUR WORD.

Selah

I am not whining, Lord. Within the realm of men, aside from Jesus, I have suffered much, though not as some have. Still, I don't see a way out of it. I don't see a way around it. I don't even think I can get through it.

That is until I remember that You took all my pain, suffering, and wounds so that I might be healed. That I *am* healed by Your stripes. There is no maybe about it.

I have to fall back on Your promise that all things work together for those who love You. I do love You, so it is a comfort to know that I am called to Your purposes in seeking my healing. What a testimony I will have, Lord. Thank You.

I glorify You and pray in Your name, Jesus.

89. ISAIAH 46:4 NIV

Even to your old age and gray hairs I am He, I am He who will sustain you. I have made you and I will carry you; I will sustain you and I will rescue you.

Selah

Your promises of old still hold true, Lord. You do not change nor do You go back on Your promised goodness.

How much I appreciate that You made me and carry me. How I glorify You that You are the One who sustains me. No person on this earth can do for me what You do. Your lovingkindness is everlasting.

There are no words to express how much I need rescuing right now, but You know all things, Lord. You know right where I am.

I place myself in Your hands and by the power of Your Holy Spirit will stop wiggling when I get antsy. You know all my anxieties and You say, over and over, "Fear not!"

I lay my fears at Your feet because You care for me and will reach down to me at all times.

Thank You for Jesus. I pray in His name. Amen.

90. 1 PETER 5:8 NLT

STAY ALERT! WATCH OUT FOR YOUR GREAT ENEMY, THE DEVIL. HE PROWLS AROUND LIKE A ROARING LION, LOOKING FOR SOMEONE TO DEVOUR.

Selah

Peter knew what he was talking about, didn't he, Lord? How many times did he fail You or even speak the words from Satan when he said, "May it never be," when You were telling the disciples how You must suffer and die. If anyone knew about the roaring lion, it was Peter, wasn't it?

I, too, must be watchful, as he says here. I don't want to be lunch, breakfast, dinner, or a snack. Devouring is so total, so devasting.

I can't imagine that You would forget me, Your child if I fall prey to the enemy. I thank You that You never leave me nor forsake me. Not even when the enemy is there to eat me up.

I can see that in my need I must be extra vigilant so that I keep up my courage. You say to be strong and courageous, do not tremble, get discouraged, nor be afraid, because You are with me wherever I go.

Let me keep my eyes on You, Lord Jesus. I pray in Your mighty name, Jesus. Amen.

91. PSALM 80:17–19 NASB

Let Your hand be upon the man of Your right hand, Upon the son of man whom You made strong for Yourself. Then we will not turn back from You; Revive us, and we will call upon Your name. Lord God of armies, restore us; Make Your face shine upon us, and we will be saved.

Selah

Father, I know You are talking about Jesus here, how He is the man of Your right hand. He is the Son of Man who You made strong to overcome death and the grave. Your time has come to revive me through the everlasting sacrifice of Jesus, the man at Your right hand.

I call on Your name, my Lord God. You are the God of the armies of angels. They all obey You at Your command. No harm can befall me when Your command goes forth. I know that because I ask the protection of Your armies, I am protected from the evil one.

Revive me, Lord, that I may praise You with all my mind and all my soul and all my strength. I look forward with anticipation for Your restoration.

Thank You that You let Your face shine on me and so I am saved by the Light of Christ.

In Jesus' name, I pray. Amen.

92. MATTHEW 12:22 NLT

Then a demon-possessed man, who was blind and couldn't speak, was brought to Jesus. He healed the man so that he could both speak and see.

Selah

Hello again, Lord Jesus, my sweet Savior. As I read of Your mighty deeds, I am astounded that You can do such works even before Your death and resurrection. You always carried the Father in You and did His will.

A poor demon-possessed man who was blind and unable to utter a word was no difficulty for You. You healed this man so that he could speak and see. What great love the Father has for His people, Israel.

You have this same love for me because I have been grafted into the vine of Jesus. Yes, I may be being pruned so that I bring forth much fruit. Yes, You see me in the midst of my pains and sorrows. You never forget me, though. You are right here with me, always.

I thank You, Jesus. Amen.

93. ACTS 9: 36–37, 40–42 NIV

In Joppa there was a disciple named Tabitha (in Greek her name is Dorcas); she was always doing good and helping the poor. About that time, she became sick and died, and her body was washed and placed in an upstairs room.

Peter sent them all out of the room; then he got down on his knees and prayed. Turning toward the dead woman, he said, "Tabitha, get up." She opened her eyes, and seeing Peter, she sat up. He took her by the hand and helped her to her feet. Then he called for the believers, especially the widows, and presented her to them alive. This became known all over Joppa, and many people believed in the Lord.

Selah

Tabitha, was a godly woman who had passed away, and her friends sent for Peter. He went in, and when he came out, she was alive! The power of the Holy Spirit was on him, and he performed a great miracle. Like Jesus, he did what the Father was doing by the mighty working of God.

He called the believers to bear witness, and they spread the word that Tabitha rose from the dead. What a testimony to all those who needed to know about Jesus and His wonderous work through Peter!

Lord, I pray that I will be raised up, too. You are no respecter of persons. Please send prayer warriors to take up my cause. Let me reach out to ministries that pray for the sick. Let me not take exception to those who would help me if I ask.

May this be healing and life to my body, mind, and spirit, and that I may receive healing and wholeness. To the glory of God, in Jesus' name, I pray. Amen.

94. PSALMS 105:37 KJV

HE BROUGHT THEM FORTH ALSO WITH SILVER AND GOLD: AND THERE WAS NOT ONE FEEBLE PERSON AMONG THEIR TRIBES.

Selah

Father, You brought out a people called by Your name from the land of the enemy. Not only that, but You gave them treasure and abundant health.

You call me by Your name, too. In Jesus, I am Your righteousness. I can't say it often enough. There is such power in being Your perfection and right standing. There is no lack of silver or gold in Your kingdom. There is no sickness or death in the Kingdom of God. Your presence is all fullness of everything in creation.

You send me all the money I need to serve my needs in Your name. I have no lack of wellness or provision. I am Your child even as the tribes of Israel were. Thank You for grafting me into the vine that is the body of Jesus. I am one with You in Him.

You have chosen to be with me by Your Holy Spirit. Jesus sent Him to comfort, counsel, and give wisdom. So, there is no feebleness, weakness, nor lack of strength in Your person, dear Father. That applies to me, also, because I am I in You.

I glorify Your name, in Jesus' name. Amen.

95. EXODUS 14:13–14 BSB

But Moses told the people, "Do not be afraid. Stand firm and you will see the Lord's salvation, which He will accomplish for you today; for the Egyptians you see today, you will never see again. The Lord will fight for you; you need only to be still."

Selah

Fearless, Delivered, and Still. Such promises You made to Your people, Lord. You accomplished in a day something the Israelites did not achieve in 400 years. Even in slavery, although they numbered about 1,200,00 men and women.

You say, "Do not be afraid." You say, "Stand firm." You say You will deliver and save. You say I will never see my enemy again. You fight for *me*. All You ask of me is to be still and wait on You...to believe in You.

When I am impatient, fearful, or doubting You, let me remember how You promise to save me. Let me close my eyes and meditate on You and Your promises that You have accomplished on my behalf because You fought for my freedom. You have set me free from slavery.

So, Lord, let me stand firm in the faith, let me be sure of Your deliverance, and let my fear vanish like a puff of wind.

Oh, praise to You, my living God.

I pray in Jesus' name. Amen.

96. PROVERBS 18:14 NIV

THE HUMAN SPIRIT CAN ENDURE A SICK BODY, BUT WHO CAN BEAR A CRUSHED SPIRIT?

Selah

My spirit has been able to endure a sick body for a while now. It has been too long, and too serious for me. With Your help, by the Holy Spirit, I hang in there, but it is crushing my spirit.

I cannot bear this without Your intercession and intervention, Holy Spirit. I will take any kind. An encouraging word, a friendly smile, a visit from someone who cares for me would help. I need to accept the help You send.

When I feel rotten, I tend to neglect to be grateful for Your grace. I reject people and close my heart to what people do for me. I guess I am sometimes still waiting for my healing Bolt from the Blue to change me and heal me. I want to recognize Your gifts when You send them.

Help me, Holy Spirit, to always be thankful for Your total investment in my healing.

Help me to remember those who are being Your hands and feet here on the earth. I now proclaim appreciation for the ministry of those You send. I will open up myself to people, even when I don't want to see them. I give this reluctance over to You so that my crushed spirit can be mended.

Thank You for Your ministers and Your Holy Spirit's direction.

Praise You and I pray in Jesus' name. Amen.

97. JAMES 4: 14–15

ARE ANY OF YOU SICK? YOU SHOULD CALL FOR THE ELDERS OF THE CHURCH TO COME AND PRAY OVER YOU, ANOINTING YOU WITH OIL IN THE NAME OF THE LORD. SUCH A PRAYER OFFERED IN FAITH WILL HEAL THE SICK, AND THE LORD WILL MAKE YOU WELL. AND IF YOU HAVE COMMITTED ANY SINS, YOU WILL BE FORGIVEN.

Selah

Lord, let me call for the elders of the church. I may not been in touch for a while. I know You don't judge me for this. Still, being in a church family could be helpful right about now, no matter how reluctant I am. I believe that in Your name, elders I call will come to me. If I can't call myself, I'll ask someone who will do this for me. I believe that the church will respond if they believe in prayer for the sick and anointing with oil.

I know that there is healing in those called to this ministry. Those who have faith, may they anoint me with oil. I know that oil is important because it is a foreshadowing of the oil of the golden lampstand next to Your throne. I have confidence that this is the way You will arrange this for me. I have faith, too.

To know, again, that my sins are forgiven is such a comfort. Jesus died so that I might have life. He has provided life abundantly, living sin-free in His grace. So, forgiveness bought with blood is eternal. Thank You so much for this forgiveness.

In faith, these prayers will heal me. You never forget me in Your word. How I love You since You have an everlasting love for me. Thank You for making me well by faith.

What a loving and merciful God I serve! There is no one like You, Lord.

I pray in Jesus' incomparable name. Amen.

98. REVELATIONS 22:1 NLT

But our citizenship is in heaven. And we eagerly await a Savior from there, the Lord Jesus Christ, who, by the power that enables him to bring everything under his control, will transform our lowly bodies so that they will be like his glorious body. Then the angel showed me a river with the water of life, clear as crystal, flowing from the throne of God and of the Lamb.

Selah

Lord, I pray for Your miraculous healing. You know what I am facing. Still, I know that this earth and this flesh are temporary. I don't know how anyone else feels about this, but I am preparing myself to come to see You.

You said the 10 virgins went out to meet the Bridegroom, who I know to be You, Jesus. Only five were prepared. I want to have the oil of the Holy Spirit in my lamp so that I might be prepared, no matter what happens to me.

Each one of us has an appointment with You. Let me be ready no matter when You come. Let Your peace surround me and take all fear of leaving this body behind. I look forward to seeing You transform my lowly body into a glorious one like You have.

I want to drink from the river of the water of life that flows directly from the throne of God and the Lamb of God. All praise to You, my King.

I pray in Jesus' name. Amen.

99. TIMOTHY 1:9-10 NIV

He has saved us and called us to a holy life—not because of anything we have done but because of his own purpose and grace. This grace was given us in Christ Jesus before the beginning of time, but it has now been revealed through the appearing of our Savior, Christ Jesus, who has destroyed death and has brought life and immortality to light through the gospel.

Selah

Father God, I thank You that You have saved me and called me to a holy life.

You gave me grace. Grace, what a word filled with so much meaning that unmerited favor does not nearly cover it. It also means unearned divine assistance, virtue coming from You, sanctification through Jesus, approval, favor, pardon, kindness, mercy, clemency and courtesy. I'm speechless before Your everlasting love.

You gave all this to me before the beginning of time. It is almost unthinkable to reflect on the fact that we could not earn this. Only Jesus gives us the grace to live life because he had destroyed death and brought immortality.

Thank You that this is available through the Good News. The Good News that Jesus was sent to us and suffered and died and rose again, that we might live with Him forevermore. And we did not deserve this at all.

Thank You, Lord, for Your grace! In Jesus' name, I pray. Amen.

100. PSALM 91:15–16 BSB

When he calls out to Me, I will answer him; I will be with him in trouble. I will deliver him and honor him. With long life, I will satisfy him and show him My salvation."

Selah

I call out to You, Lord Jesus. You promise me that You will answer me. Over and over in Your word, You say You will answer me. Jesus tells us that, through Him, all we ask will be given to us. I ask for healing now and throughout the rest of my life.

I believe that You are with me in this trouble. You never leave me or forsake me. You build my faith because in this distress of mine You stand by me day and night.

Your promise to deliver me and honor me is so fantastic! How I have been troubled by the enemy. Giving me honor in the presence of the enemy fills my heart with joy and peace. Even me, who needs Your grace daily to get through.

You promise to satisfy me with a long life. You have shown me salvation and eternal life through Jesus.

101. ROMANS 8:38–39 AMP

For I am convinced [and continue to be convinced—beyond any doubt] that neither death, nor life, nor angels, nor principalities, nor things present *and* threatening, nor things to come, nor powers, nor height, nor depth, nor any other created thing, will be able to separate us from the [unlimited] love of God, which is in Christ Jesus our Lord.

Selah

Dear Father. how great is Your Love for us! Nothing, no nothing, can separate us from Your incomparable love. You are with us in death. You are with us in life. There are no spiritual forces of angels or demons, nor physical dimensions that can keep us apart.

My fears today and anxieties for tomorrow mean nothing to You because You love me, no matter what. There is no condemnation in You toward me. You just love me.

Not even the fires and torments of the pits of Hell can hold Your love for me at bay.

I know that in such love there is health and wholeness. I know that because of Your righteousness You always keep Your word. You will not let me down. I am always on Your mind and You will never forget to work the miracles You speak of all through the Bible.

Lord, I thank You for Your faithfulness and honesty.

In Jesus' name, I pray. Amen

CHAPTER EIGHT

A Prayer for Salvation

Lord Jesus, I have gone my own way and not Yours. I have missed Your mark of perfection, and the Father, because He is perfect, pure and holy requires anyone who is in his presence to be the same. Jesus, You said no one comes to the Father by through You. I am asking for Your salvation. I ask You to forgive me for all my sins by the power of Your cross.

I believe that You are the Son of God, Jesus. I know that You were also a real, born of a woman, Man. I believe that You suffered and died that I could be saved. I believe that, in You, I am the righteousness of God. I believe You have forgiven me and made me both God's child and Your friend.

You are the Son of God and God the Son. I proudly confess that I am Your own. I am free, loved, and saved. I am free from the Law of sin and death now. I am Yours and You are mine, oh, Holy Jesus.

Thank You, Jesus. Amen.

Afterword

This has been a labor of love sent to you in the glorious name of our Savior, Jesus Christ. It is my hope and prayer that you are strengthened in your inner person by this book. I pray for your healing and restoration to health and wholeness.

You can send your prayer requests and praise reports to similarsister@elliseanhouse.com.

I have a gift for you, too. An e-book telling my backstory. Since I use a pen name for publishing, this will give you a little about me, my journey, and how I came to write this book.

Additionally, I have created bookmarks for you to laminate with my five favorite Scriptures from the book. These make perfect little gifts and reminders of God's love for us and His healing grace.

My final special gift is a recording of all the Scriptures this book in my own voice.

These Words of God are healing and life to all who hear them, according the Holy Scripture. You will be able to listen even when you are not able to read. This is not an Audible book. That will include the prayers and music with a professional narrator. This is my heart, gifting this reading for you. These are the Scriptures of God for you to return to, and continue in God's incomparable gift, surpassing all others by bringing perfect peace, healing and wholeness.

I send these to you in the mighty name of Jesus.

Just send your request to similarsister@elliseanhouse.com.

Please know that your private information is just that, private. I will never break the sacred trust you have placed in me. Your name and email will never be shared, sold or in any way leave my possession. I want you to be perfectly assured of the safety of your information.

As an added bonus for you! I would like to send you a beautiful personalized graphic, suitable for framing. Send me the scripture from the 101 to choose from in the book that you want, and I will send the scripture picture back to you for printing. It is my hope this will be a faith builder for you or a friend and a reminder of God's love and power.

Also, if you are interested in becoming a prayer partner, or a beta reader, please let me know at my email address.

I would be happy to visit your church to speak and pray over the sick. Just make your request and we can discuss a visit.

I appreciate hearing any response you have. You can always write to me for personal notes, but if you want to leave any comments you have regarding the book, it can be rated the Audible, or Amazon Paperback rating sections. Ratings are how others choose how to make a decision for their purchase. You can influence other readers with your thoughts on this work. I am grateful for your response.

In His eternal love,
A Similar Sister
similarsister@elliseanhouse.com

Made in the USA
Middletown, DE
11 February 2023